The American Collection

RANCH STYLE

200 House Plan

D1288488

Open Layouts, Single-Level Living, Affordable Design

The American Collection

RANCH STYLE

hanley▲wood

Published by Hanley Wood
One Thomas Circle, NW, Suite 600
Washington, DC 20005

Distribution Center
PBD
Hanley Wood Consumer Group
3280 Summit Ridge Parkway
Duluth, Georgia 30096

Vice President, Home Plans, Andrew Schultz
Director, Marketing, Mark Wilkin
Associate Publisher, Development, Jennifer Pearce
Editor, Simon Hyoun
Assistant Editor, Kimberly Johnson
Publications Manager, Brian Haefs
Production Manager, Theresa Emerson
Senior Plan Merchandiser, Nicole Phipps
Plan Merchandiser, Hillary Huff
Graphic Artist, Joong Min
Product Manager, Susan Jasmin
Marketing Manager, Brett Bryant

Most Hanley Wood titles are available at quantity discounts with bulk purchases for educational, business, or sales promotional use. For information, please contact Andrew Schultz at aschultz@hanleywood.com.

VC Graphics, Inc.
Creative Director, Veronica Vannoy
Graphic Designer, Jennifer Gerstein
Graphic Designer, Denise Reiffenstein
Graphic Designer, Jeanne-Erin Worster

Photo Credits
Front Cover Main Image: HPK3300001 on page 8, photo by Bob Greenspan, courtesy of Alan Mascord Designs, Inc.
Front Cover Inset and Back Cover Top Images: HPK3300109 on page 75, photo by Bob Greenspan, courtesy of Home Planners.
Back Cover Bottom: HPK3300184 on page 137, photo courtesy of William E. Poole Designs, Inc. Wilmington NC.

10 9 8 7 6 5 4 3 2 1

Printed in the United States of America

Library of Congress Control Number: 2006935047

ISBN-10: 1-931131-74-0
ISBN-13: 978-1-931131-74-2

The American Collection
RANCH STYLE

6

CONTENTS

ONLINE EXTRA!

PASSAGEWAY

For access to bonus home plans, articles,
online ordering, and more go to: **www.hanley
woodbooks.com/acranchstyle**

Features of this site include:

- A dynamic link that lets you search and
  view bonus home plans
- Online related feature articles
- Built-in tools to save and view your favorite
  home plans
- A dynamic web link that allows you to
  order your home plan online
- Contact details for the Hanley Wood Home
  Plan Hotline
- Free subscriptions to Hanley Wood Home
  Plan e-news

hanley▲wood

THE NEW RANCH

Make a mark on the present with a house plan from the past

Since the 1930s, ranch-style homes have been staples of the American suburbs. Modeled after the single-level designs of the rural west, they began as affordable housing for the working class and became the "it" house of the 1950s and 1960s. Today, they are the foundation for many more contemporary designs as well as nostalgic throw-back homes. Join *The American Collection: Ranch Style* as it traces this housing trend through the decades and provides section after section of ranch-style house plans.

The front door of this ranch opens almost directly to an open-plan living room. See the floor plan on page 102.

A brick-and-stone facade plus classical columns give this ranch traditional appeal. See the floor plan on page 63.

Ranch Basics

A typical ranch home is one level with an asymmetrical, streamlined shape. It's longer than it is deep and has very simple rooflines—usually a side-gable, sometimes a cross-gable for a side- or front-loading garage. The minimalist design makes this style of home extremely affordable, therefore vinyl siding is a popular exterior, but it can be easily embellished with brick or stone accents. Many of the house plans included in this book fit this description to a T, but designers have also chosen to take this basic form and run with it. For example, a ranch home can have a long footprint with any type of material on the facade, clerestory dormers for the appearance of a second floor, or a wrapping front porch; a modern modified ranch can even have a basement foundation. Current ranch homes can meet the layout demands of today, while still paying homage to the ranches of yesterday.

Home on the Ranch

The affordability and flexibility of ranch homes allows you to locate them anywhere. In New England, vinyl siding may be the exterior preference, but in the Southwest, stucco is more suitable. You can find a ranch home plan in this book with either of these materials and more. Found a house plan you love but are challenged by a hillside lot? Our customization service can turn any foundation into a walkout basement; and from the front, the home will still resemble the ranches we love.

How to Use This Book

Following this introduction, our featured homes section will take you on a tour of two designs that exemplify a modern ranch home. Take time to visualize the flow of interior spaces and imagine how these homes—and others like them—would feel to you. The rest of the book is divided into three sections and ordered by square footage. Every plan discussed in this book is available to own. Turn to page 184 to learn how to order a plan and what you will receive with your purchase. Materials lists, customization, home automation, and other options are also explained in this part of the book, followed by the list of prices on page 190.

The shingle-and-siding facade is a distinctly New England look that adds rusticity and style.

A Ranch by any Other Name

Different styles come together to beautify a ranch home

Multiple gables, front columns, and square windows reveal a combination of Colonial, country, and Craftsman influences upon this ranch home. A facade of siding and shingles recommend it to northern locations, particularly in New England, where Cape Cod is the style of choice.

Inside, a great room is the focal point of a house plan with a room in each of the four corners. The front two are occupied by a den on the right and a bedroom on the left. The back left corner houses the spacious island kitchen and dining area with a French door to the rear porch. In the rear right corner, a master bedroom accesses a private porch. The suite is complete with a large walk-in closet and a luxurious bath with a corner shower.

A good example of a modern modified ranch, this plan includes a finished basement. Downstairs, the two remaining bedrooms share space with a media room, large rec room with a fireplace, and plenty of space for storage.

Main Level

3 CAR GARAGE
23'6"x35'0"

PORCH
9'0"x10'0"

DIN.
WOOD BEAM
CATHEDRAL CEILING
16'0"x12'0"

PORCH
24'0"x8'0"

MBR.
CATHEDRAL CEILING
14'0"x18'4"

PORCH
11'0"x10'6"

GRT. RM.
WOOD BEAM
CATHEDRAL CEILING
19'8"x18'8"

KIT.
10'-1 1/2" CEILING
14'6"x15'0"

PAN.

E
CATHEDRAL CEILING

BR. #2
10'-1 1/2" CEILING
14'6"x12'0"

DEN
10'-1 1/2" CEILING
14'0"x13'0"

Lower Level

13'8"x11'8"

BR. #4
9'-1 1/2" CEILING
14'0"x12'4"

STOR.

STOR.

REC. RM.
9'-1 1/2" STEP CEILING
35'8"x19'0"

BR. #3
9'-1 1/2" CEILING
16'0"x13'4"

MEDIA RM.
9'-1 1/2" CEILING
16'0"x22'2"

WET BAR

STOR.

PLAN:

HPK3300033

MAIN LEVEL:
2,551 sq. ft.

LOWER LEVEL:
2,028 sq. ft.

TOTAL:
4,579 sq. ft.

BEDROOMS:
4

BATHROOMS:
3

WIDTH:
89' - 4"

DEPTH:
67' - 0"

FOUNDATION:
Finished Basement

Order online at eplans.com

Above: Light, romantic fabrics set a relaxing tone in the vaulted master bedroom.

Below: In the kitchen, a central snack-bar island offers cabinets and counter space, while a Craftsman-style divider provides even more storage.

the actual blueprints. For more detailed information, please check the floor plans carefully.

A Prairie
HOME ESTATE

*Where every room
is extraordinary*

Exposed beams and stone reinforce the
home's Prairie-style influence.

Left: The master bedroom has tall glass doors and windows that face the private rear of the home and shares a through fireplace with the master bath.

This ranch home is fashioned with a heavy Prairie-style influence, which lends itself easily to streamlined modern décor.

The sprawling design is a wide 165 feet, with four wings spurring from a central hub of formal and casual spaces. These common rooms include a foyer and living room, with an office and guest room on one side and a dining room and kitchen with nook on the other.

The right side of the home consists of a three-car garage followed by a wing of relaxed entertainment areas: a family room, game room, porch, and studio. Sleeping quarters are on the left side of the plan. In the front wing, three bedrooms and three baths surround a play room, ideal for families. To the rear, the master suite is finished with a galley walk-in closet with two entrances and a luxurious bath complete with standing shower and garden tub.

The hearth-warmed bedroom directly accesses a rear porch that spans the width of the house and borders a fountain-dotted pool. Varying levels help define entertainment zones that easily accommodate groups, large or small.

Right: The dining room is immediately to the right of the foyer, whose art niche and interesting lighting make a strong first impression.

Above: A peninsula fireplace in the family room warms the space and provides partial separation from the game room.

Right: Simple furnishings and minimal decorations add elegance to the formal dining room.

AFFORDABLE BEGINNINGS

A small ranch design is the perfect starter home for a young couple, new family, or empty-nesters. Its size and materials make it affordable, and its shape suits it to a smaller lot. The style is simple—with clean lines that lend it to modern trends or traditional accents—which also creates a blank canvas for attractive landscaping.

In less than 2,000 square feet, a family could have a sun-filled eat-in kitchen near a sliding glass door to a back patio. The kitchen itself may be a galley or even have an island or peninsula. An open layout between this room and a family room will maximize space and make the area feel larger than its square footage. Nearby, a long hallway can lead from a casual living room or family room to up to three bedrooms, allowing space for a guest room or home office.

A home of this size isn't without ample storage space. Basement foundations contain plenty of unfinished or finished room for seasonal and over-sized items. A garage can easily house equipment and boxes with help from shelving systems and cabinetry. And, if this isn't enough space, go to eplans.com to order plans for outdoor projects, such as storage and gardening sheds.

PLAN:
HPK3300034

SQUARE FOOTAGE:
1,883

BEDROOMS:
3

BATHROOMS:
2

WIDTH:
68' - 8"

DEPTH:
41' - 8"

FOUNDATION:
Unfinished Basement

Order online at eplans.com

An appealing plan to passersby, this design makes a practical starter home for first-time builders. With a great use of space, the designer aptly fit three bedrooms and two full baths on one floor, using less than 1,900 square feet. A home office near the front door easily converts to a fourth bedroom if needed.

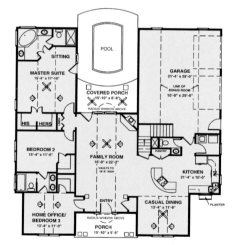

Rear Exterior

PLAN:
HPK3300035

SQUARE FOOTAGE:
1,725

BEDROOMS:
2

BATHROOMS:
2

WIDTH:
64' - 0"

DEPTH:
53' - 6"

FOUNDATION:
Crawlspace

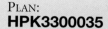
Order online at eplans.com

PLAN:
HPK3300036

SQUARE FOOTAGE:
1,798

BEDROOMS:
3

BATHROOMS:
2 ½

WIDTH:
54' - 0"

DEPTH:
56' - 2"

FOUNDATION:
Slab

Order online at eplans.com

PLAN:
HPK3300037

SQUARE FOOTAGE:
1,850

BEDROOMS:
3

BATHROOMS:
2

WIDTH:
44' - 0"

DEPTH:
68' - 0"

FOUNDATION:
Crawlspace

Order online at eplans.com

With all of the tantalizing elements of a cottage and the comfortable space of a family-sized home, this Arts and Crafts one-story is the best of both worlds. Exterior accents, such as stone wainscot, cedar shingles under the gable ends, and mission-style windows, enhance this effect. Three bedrooms are aligned along the right of the interior, situated behind the garage, shielding them from street noise. Bedroom 3 and the master bedroom have walk-in closets; a tray ceiling decorates the master salon. Living and dining areas include a large great room, a dining room with sliding glass doors to a rear patio, and a private den with window seat and vaulted ceiling. A warming hearth lights the great room—right next to a built-in media center. The open corner kitchen features a 42-inch snack bar counter and giant walk-in pantry.

PLAN:
HPK3300038

There's a lot packed into this traditional one-story home—from the three bedrooms to the magnificent combined kitchen, breakfast nook, and family room. A curved cooktop island adds a thoughtful touch to the kitchen's efficiency and the family-room fireplace will surely make this area the center of family activity. Adjoining living and dining rooms placed toward the front of the home will bring many memorable evenings entertaining friends. The fabulous master suite boasts an ample walk-in closet and a private bath with a twin-sink vanity, shower, and tub. The other two bedrooms, set on the other side of the house, share a bath. The laundry room is off the kitchen entry to the garage.

SQUARE FOOTAGE:
1,699
BEDROOMS:
3
BATHROOMS:
2
WIDTH:
50' - 0"
DEPTH:
51' - 0"
FOUNDATION:
Crawlspace

Order online at eplans.com

PLAN:
HPK3300039

SQUARE FOOTAGE:
1,728

BEDROOMS:
2

BATHROOMS:
2

WIDTH:
55' - 0"

DEPTH:
48' - 0"

FOUNDATION:
Crawlspace

Order online at eplans.com

A charming dormer window accents the facade of this cozy Craftsman home. To the left of the foyer, double doors open to a den; choose built-in shelves or a convenient wall closet for this room. The central great room boasts a vaulted ceiling, built-in media center, and fireplace, and is open to the dining room, which features sliding glass doors that open to a side porch. A built-in desk adds convenience to the kitchen. Bedrooms to the left of the plan include a master suite, with a private bath and walk-in closet, and one additional bedroom.

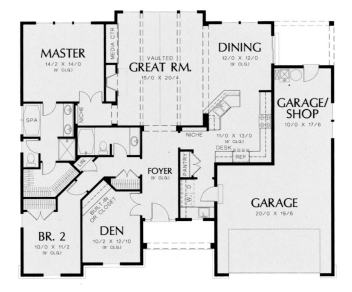

PLAN:

HPK3300040

SQUARE FOOTAGE:
1,873
BEDROOMS:
3
BATHROOMS:
2
WIDTH:
70' - 0"
DEPTH:
51' - 6"
FOUNDATION:
Crawlspace

Order online at eplans.com

Arches and pillars invite you to step onto the front covered porch and enter this magnificent ranch house. A C-shaped kitchen with a cooktop island counter flows into the dining area, which opens through French doors to the back patio. Open space between the dining room and the great room helps enhance the sense of expansive living area. Art niches next to the fireplace dress up this room that will be the focal point of family gatherings and social occasions. The master suite, with all the comforts you need for soothing relaxation, sits next to a den that could also serve as a study or library. Two other bedrooms share a bath. The two-car garage has extra space to park a motorcycle or garden tractor, or for making a workshop.

PLAN:
HPK3300041

SQUARE FOOTAGE:
1,557

BEDROOMS:
3

BATHROOMS:
2

WIDTH:
50' - 0"

DEPTH:
50' - 0"

FOUNDATION:
Crawlspace

Order online at eplans.com

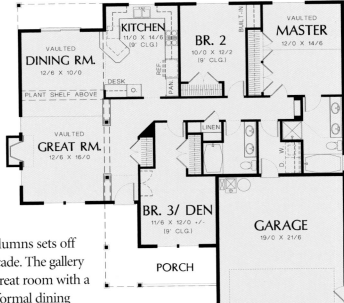

A railed porch with columns sets off this sweet country facade. The gallery foyer opens to a vaulted great room with a fireplace and leads to the formal dining room. Advanced amenities such as a vaulted ceiling and a plant shelf complement views of nature through tall windows and sliding glass doors. A planning desk, pantry, and peninsula counter highlight the gourmet kitchen, which boasts a window over the sink. A flex room easily converts from a secondary bedroom to a den or home office. A second bedroom offers a view of the rear property; nearby, a full bath includes two vanity sinks.

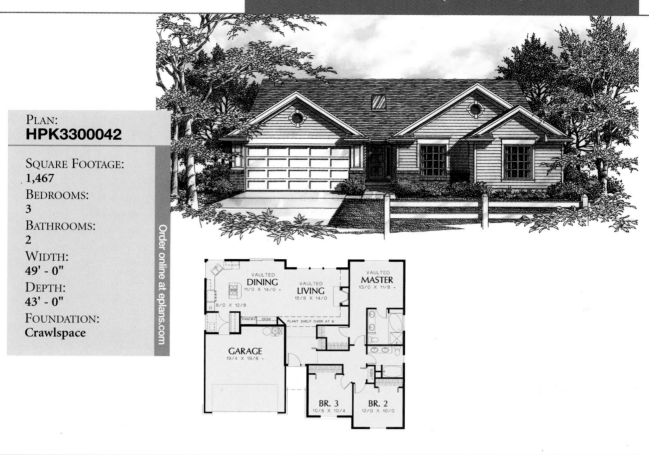

PLAN:
HPK3300042

SQUARE FOOTAGE:
1,467

BEDROOMS:
3

BATHROOMS:
2

WIDTH:
49' - 0"

DEPTH:
43' - 0"

FOUNDATION:
Crawlspace

Order online at eplans.com

PLAN:
HPK3300043

SQUARE FOOTAGE:
1,997

BEDROOMS:
4

BATHROOMS:
2 ½

WIDTH:
60' - 0"

DEPTH:
51' - 0"

FOUNDATION:
Crawlspace

Order online at eplans.com

© Larry E. Belk Designs

PLAN:
HPK3300044

SQUARE FOOTAGE:
1,170

BEDROOMS:
3

BATHROOMS:
2

WIDTH:
51' - 10"

DEPTH:
53' - 6"

FOUNDATION:
Crawlspace, Slab

Order online at eplans.com

Timeless appeal is the hallmark of this charming traditional home with its sheltering porch that extends a gracious welcome. Inside, the foyer opens directly to a living room highlighted by a corner fireplace. To the right, enter the bayed dining room and enjoy the natural light that also fills the kitchen. A built-in desk simplifies meal planning, and windows over the sink open up views of the covered porch and front property. The master suite will please with its large walk-in closet and compartmented bath. Two family bedrooms both have spacious closets.

© Larry E. Belk Designs

GARAGE

STORAGE

MSTR BDRM
11–0x13–8
10 FT CLG

MSTR BATH

LIVING
13–0x17–8
10 FT CLG

DESK

DINING
11–0x
9–2

BATH 2

STOR

FOYER

KITCH
11–6x
8–0

LIN

BDRM 3
10–10x11–6

BDRM 2
10–4x10–2

COVERED PORCH

© Larry E. Belk Designs

At first glance, you may notice how the covered front porch, shutters, and flowering window boxes dress up this home, but it's more than just a pretty face. Enter the combined kitchen/dining room where amenities include a bay window and a built-in desk. A corner fireplace warms the living room while French doors provide access to the backyard. Located to the rear, the master suite features a private bath and walk-in closet. Two family bedrooms share a full bath.

PLAN:
HPK3300045

SQUARE FOOTAGE:
1,202
BEDROOMS:
3
BATHROOMS:
2
WIDTH:
51' - 10"
DEPTH:
43' - 10"
FOUNDATION:
Crawlspace, Slab

Order online at eplans.com

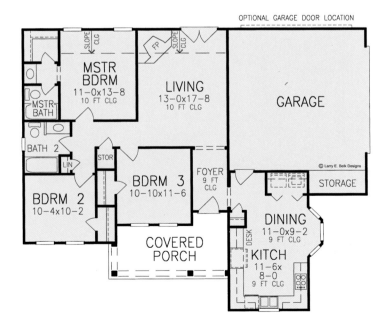

© Larry E. Belk Designs

PLAN:
HPK3300046

SQUARE FOOTAGE:
1,772

BEDROOMS:
3

BATHROOMS:
2

WIDTH:
45' - 8"

DEPTH:
50' - 2"

FOUNDATION:
Crawlspace, Slab

Order online at eplans.com

A folk Victorian flair gives this home its curb appeal. Inside, a large living room boasts a centerpiece fireplace and a coffered ceiling. The kitchen has a 42-inch-high breakfast bar and a pantry. The master suite includes a 10-foot coffered ceiling and a luxury bath with a corner whirlpool tub, separate shower, His and Hers vanities, and a roomy walk-in closet. Two additional bedrooms and a bath are nearby. A two-car garage plan is included with this design and can be connected to the home with a breezeway.

© Larry E. Belk Designs

A finely detailed covered porch and arch-topped windows announce a scrupulously designed interior, replete with amenities. A grand foyer with a 10-foot ceiling and columned archways set the pace for the entire floor plan. Clustered sleeping quarters to the left feature a deluxe master suite with a sloped ceiling, corner whirlpool bath, and walk-in closet; as well as two family bedrooms that share a bath. Picture windows flanking a centered fireplace lend plenty of natural light to the great room, which is open through grand columned archways to the formal dining area and the bay-windowed breakfast room.

PLAN:
HPK3300047

SQUARE FOOTAGE:
1,955
BEDROOMS:
3
BATHROOMS:
2
WIDTH:
65' - 0"
DEPTH:
58' - 8"
FOUNDATION:
Crawlspace, Slab

Order online at eplans.com

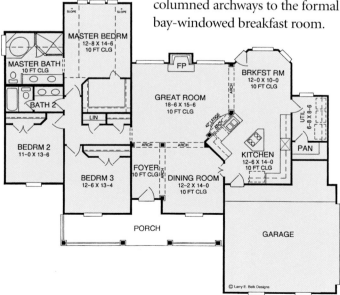

PLAN:
HPK3300048

SQUARE FOOTAGE:
1,973

BEDROOMS:
3

BATHROOMS:
2

WIDTH:
74' - 2"

DEPTH:
44' - 10"

FOUNDATION:
Crawlspace, Slab

Order online at eplans.com

An angled entry is defined by arches and columns, giving this traditional home an elegant flavor. This split bedroom plan offers privacy for the master suite, which opens just off the foyer through double doors and offers a sumptuous bath with angled garden tub, knee-space vanity, twin lavatories, and a walk-in closet with dressing area. Family bedrooms are clustered to the left of the plan and share a hall bath. Decorative archways grace entrances to the great room, which offers an impressive fireplace flanked by windows, giving views to the rear grounds. The nearby kitchen with angled counter and walk-in pantry opens to a bright breakfast room with triple windows.

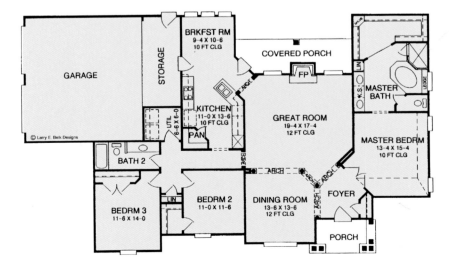

© Larry E. Belk Designs

A gabled roof flanked by attractive dormers tops the welcoming covered front porch of this country charmer. Inside, a formal dining room opens directly off the foyer, announced by decorative columns. The nearby living room offers a warming fireplace and access to the rear covered porch. Angled counters in the kitchen contribute to easy food preparation, while a snack counter accommodates quick meals. Nestled in its own wing, the master suite opens through double doors from a private vestibule and offers a relaxing retreat for the homeowner. On the other side of the plan, two family bedrooms share a full hall bath.

PLAN:
HPK3300049

SQUARE FOOTAGE:
1,993
BONUS SPACE:
307 sq. ft.
BEDROOMS:
3
BATHROOMS:
2
WIDTH:
66' - 10"
DEPTH:
71' - 5"
FOUNDATION:
Crawlspace, Slab

Order online at eplans.com

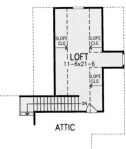

COPYRIGHT LARRY E. BELK

HOLZHAUER INC.

PLAN:
HPK3300050

SQUARE FOOTAGE:
1,504

BEDROOMS:
3

BATHROOMS:
2

WIDTH:
55' - 2"

DEPTH:
46' - 10"

FOUNDATION:
Crawlspace, Slab

Order online at eplans.com

A sunburst-window motif runs the length of this pretty, contemporary home. Enter to find wonderful ceiling treatments throughout; a coffered ceiling in the great room and vaulted ceilings in the master bedroom and Bedroom 3. Tucked away at the back of the home, the kitchen and dining area allow free movement between rooms for ease of serving. The master suite includes an ample closet and a bath with a tub window. Two additional bedrooms share a hall bath and a convenient hall linen closet. Note the optional covered porch/patio for outdoor fun.

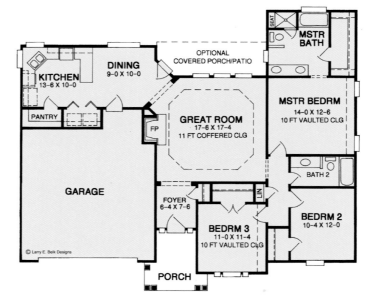

© Larry E. Belk Designs

This charming traditional has all the amenities of a larger plan in a compact layout. Ten-foot ceilings give this home an expansive feel. An angled eating bar separates the kitchen from the great room while leaving these areas open to one another for family gatherings and entertaining. The master bedroom includes a huge walk-in closet and a superior master bath with a whirlpool tub and separate shower. A large utility room and an oversized storage area are located near the secondary entrance to the home. Two additional bedrooms and a bath finish the plan.

PLAN:
HPK3300051

SQUARE FOOTAGE:
1,862

BEDROOMS:
3

BATHROOMS:
2

WIDTH:
65' - 0"

DEPTH:
46' - 2"

FOUNDATION:
Crawlspace, Slab

Order online at eplans.com

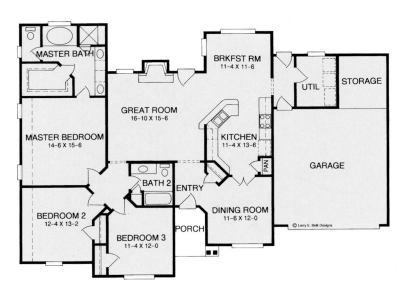

© Larry E. Belk Designs

PLAN:
HPK3300052

SQUARE FOOTAGE:
1,742

BEDROOMS:
3

BATHROOMS:
2

WIDTH:
78' - 10"

DEPTH:
40' - 10"

FOUNDATION:
Crawlspace, Slab

Order online at eplans.com

This traditional design warmly welcomes both family and visitors with a delightful bay window, a Palladian window, and shutters. The entry introduces a beautiful interior plan, starting with the formal dining room, the central great room with a fireplace, views, and access to outdoor spaces. Ten-foot ceilings in the major living areas give the home an open, spacious feel. The kitchen features an angled eating bar, a pantry, and lots of cabinet and counter space. Comfort and style abound in the distinctive master suite, offering a high ceiling, corner whirlpool tub, knee-space vanity, and compartmented toilet. An ample walk-in closet with a window for natural light completes this retreat. Nearby, Bedrooms 2 and 3 share a hall bath, and Bedroom 3 offers a raised ceiling.

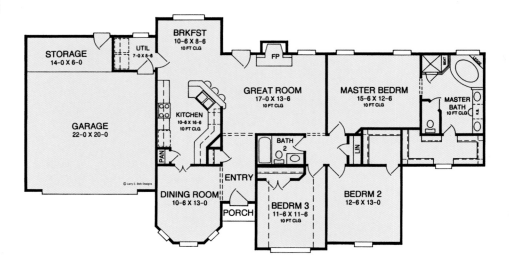

PLAN:
HPK3300053

SQUARE FOOTAGE:
1,890
BEDROOMS:
3
BATHROOMS:
2
WIDTH:
65' - 10"
DEPTH:
53' - 5"
FOUNDATION:
Crawlspace, Slab

Order online at eplans.com

This classic home exudes elegance and style and offers sophisticated amenities in a compact size. Ten-foot ceilings throughout the plan lend an aura of spacious hospitality. A generous living room with a sloped ceiling, built-in bookcases, and a centerpiece fireplace offers views as well as access to the rear yard. The nearby breakfast room shares an informal eating counter with the ample kitchen, which serves the coffer-ceilinged dining room through French doors. Three bedrooms include a sumptuous master suite with windowed whirlpool tub and walk-in closet, and two family bedrooms that share a full bath.

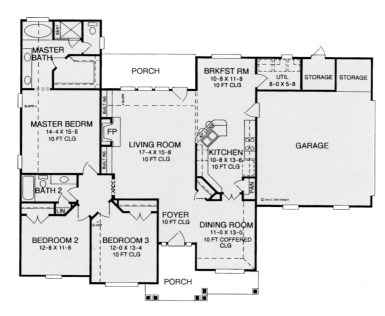

PLAN:
HPK3300054

SQUARE FOOTAGE:
1,520

BEDROOMS:
3

BATHROOMS:
2

WIDTH:
62' - 0"

DEPTH:
36' - 0"

FOUNDATION:
Unfinished Basement

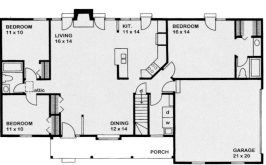

BEDROOM 11 x 10 | LIVING 16 x 14 | KIT. 11 x 14 | BEDROOM 16 x 14
attic
BEDROOM 11 x 10 | DINING 12 x 14 | d w | PORCH | GARAGE 21 x 20

Master Bdrm. 13⁶ x 15⁰ Tray Cell. | Brkfst. 9⁴ x 9⁴ | Sundeck
M Bath | Kit. 11⁴ x 12² | Living Area 17¹⁰ x 15⁶ 12' High Cell. | Bdrm.3 11⁶ x 11⁶
Dbl. Garage 19⁸ x 21⁸ | Dining 11⁴ x 13⁶ | Foyer 6'0 x 8'0 12' High Cell. | Bdrm.2 11⁶ x 13⁶

PLAN:
HPK3300055

SQUARE FOOTAGE:
1,787

BEDROOMS:
3

BATHROOMS:
2 ½

WIDTH:
64' - 0"

DEPTH:
52' - 0"

FOUNDATION:
Unfinished Walkout Basement

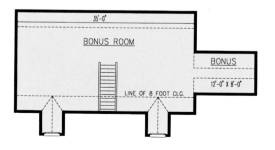

Perfectly symmetrical on the outside, this appealing home has an equally classic floor plan on the inside. A covered porch featuring full multipane windows opens directly to the spacious great room, which is open to the dining room and U-shaped kitchen for convenience and gracious entertaining. The kitchen connects to a roomy utility room with loads of counter space and windows overlooking the rear yard. The master suite lies to the front of the plan and has a view of the covered porch and a luxurious bath. Two family bedrooms reside to the rear of the plan; each has a window with backyard views.

PLAN:
HPK3300056

SQUARE FOOTAGE:
1,512
BONUS SPACE:
555 sq. ft.
BEDROOMS:
3
BATHROOMS:
2
WIDTH:
60' - 0"
DEPTH:
38' - 0"
FOUNDATION:
Crawlspace, Unfinished Basement

Order online at eplans.com

PLAN:
HPK3300057

SQUARE FOOTAGE:
1,366
BEDROOMS:
3
BATHROOMS:
2
WIDTH:
71' - 4"
DEPTH:
35' - 10"
FOUNDATION:
**Crawlspace, Slab,
Unfinished Basement**

Order online at eplans.com

A quiet, aesthetically pleasant, and comfortable one-story country home answers the requirements of modest-income families. The entrance to the house is sheltered by the front porch, which leads to the hearth-warmed living room. The master suite is arranged with a large dressing area that has a walk-in closet, plus two linear closets and space for a vanity. The main part of the bedroom contains a media center. The adjoining, fully equipped kitchen includes the dinette that can comfortably seat six people and leads to the rear terrace through 6-foot sliding glass doors.

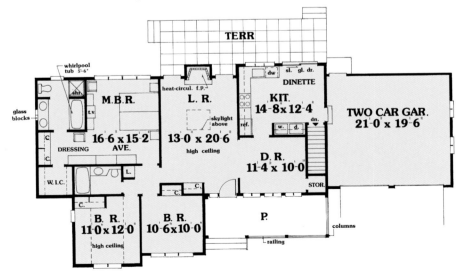

PLAN:

HPK3300058

SQUARE FOOTAGE:
1,868
BEDROOMS:
3
BATHROOMS:
2
WIDTH:
72' - 0"
DEPTH:
42' - 0"
FOUNDATION:
Unfinished Basement

Order online at eplans.com

A large living area dominates the center of this contemporary-flavored traditional one-story. It opens off of a vaulted foyer through a doorway with soffit. At one end is a warming hearth; at the other, another soffitted opening to the dining area and island kitchen. The dining area is enhanced by a bay window with sliding glass doors to the outdoors. The bedrooms are at the opposite end of the plan and include two family bedrooms and a master suite. Accents in the master suite: a corner shower, whirlpool tub, double sinks, a large walk-in closet, and a sliding glass door to the rear yard.

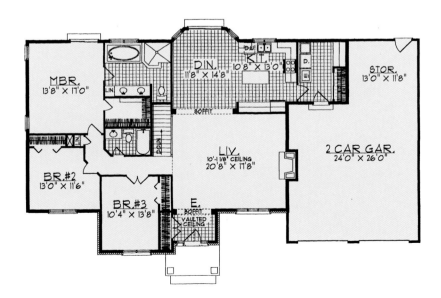

PLAN:
HPK3300059

SQUARE FOOTAGE:
1,836
BEDROOMS:
3
BATHROOMS:
2
WIDTH:
65' - 8"
DEPTH:
55' - 0"
FOUNDATION:
Crawlspace, Slab, Unfinished Basement

Order online at eplans.com

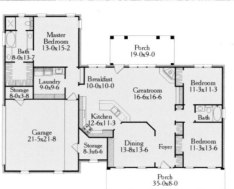

PLAN:
HPK3300060

SQUARE FOOTAGE:
1,688
BEDROOMS:
3
BATHROOMS:
2
WIDTH:
70' - 1"
DEPTH:
48' - 0"
FOUNDATION:
Crawlspace, Slab, Unfinished Basement

Order online at eplans.com

The wide front steps, columned porch, and symmetrical layout give this charming home a Georgian appeal. The large kitchen, with its walk-in pantry, island snack bar, and breakfast nook, will gratify any cook. The central great room offers radiant French doors on both sides of the fireplace. Outside those doors is a comfortable covered porch with two skylights. To the left of the great room reside four bedrooms—three secondary bedrooms and a master bedroom. The master bedroom includes a walk-in closet, twin-vanity sinks, a separate shower and tub, and private access to the rear porch.

PLAN:
HPK3300061

SQUARE FOOTAGE:
1,997
BEDROOMS:
4
BATHROOMS:
2 ½
WIDTH:
56' - 4"
DEPTH:
67' - 4"
FOUNDATION:
Crawlspace, Slab, Unfinished Basement

Order online at eplans.com

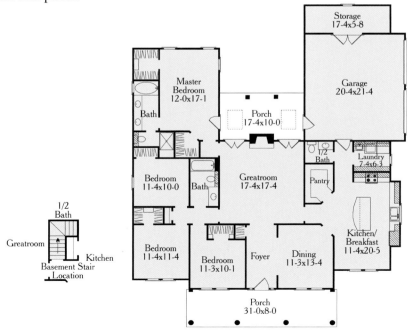

PLAN:
HPK3300062

SQUARE FOOTAGE:
1,864

BONUS SPACE:
420 sq. ft.

BEDROOMS:
3

BATHROOMS:
2 ½

WIDTH:
71' - 0"

DEPTH:
56' - 4"

Order online at eplans.com

Quaint and cozy on the outside with porches front and back, this three-bedroom country home surprises with an open floor plan featuring a large great room with a cathedral ceiling. A central kitchen with an angled counter opens to the breakfast and great rooms for easy entertaining. The privately located master bedroom features a cathedral ceiling and access to the deck. Two secondary bedrooms share a full hall bath. A bonus room makes expanding easy.

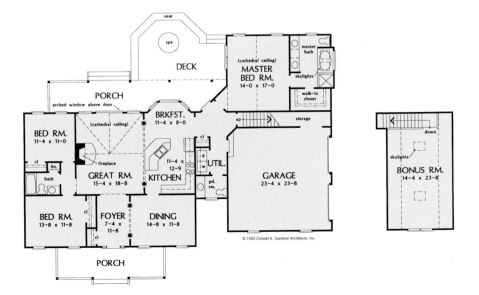

© 1993 Donald A. Gardner Architects, Inc.

PLAN:
HPK3300063

SQUARE FOOTAGE:
1,737
BEDROOMS:
3
BATHROOMS:
2
WIDTH:
65' - 10"
DEPTH:
59' - 8"

Order online at eplans.com

Inviting porches are just the beginning of this lovely country home. To the left of the foyer, a columned entry supplies a classic touch to a spacious great room that features a cathedral ceiling, built-in bookshelves, and a fireplace that invites you to share its warmth. An octagonal dining room with a tray ceiling provides a perfect setting for formal occasions. The adjacent kitchen is designed to easily serve both formal and informal areas. It includes an island cooktop and a built-in pantry, with the sunny breakfast area just a step away. The master suite, separated from two family bedrooms by the walk-in closet and utility room, offers privacy and comfort.

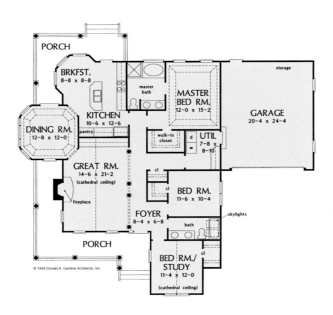

© 1994 Donald A. Gardner Architects, Inc.

PLAN:
HPK3300064

SQUARE FOOTAGE:
1,977

BONUS SPACE:
430 sq. ft.

BEDROOMS:
3

BATHROOMS:
2

WIDTH:
69' - 8"

DEPTH:
59' - 6"

Order online at eplans.com

A two-story foyer with a Palladian window above sets the tone for this sunlit home. Columns mark the passage from the foyer to the great room, where a central fireplace and built-in cabinets stretch the length of one wall. A screened porch with four skylights and a wet bar provides a pleasant place to start the day or wind down after work. The kitchen is flanked by the formal dining room and the breakfast room. Hidden quietly at the rear, the master suite includes a bath with dual vanities and skylights. Two family bedrooms (one an optional study) share a bath with twin sinks.

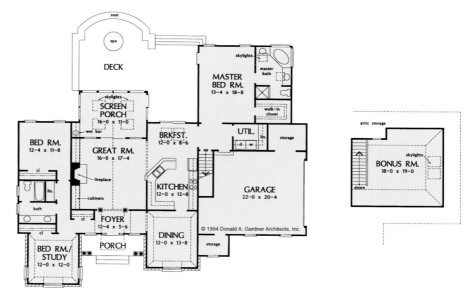

PLAN:
HPK3300065

This charming country plan boasts a cathedral ceiling in the great room. Dormer windows shed light on the foyer, which opens to a front bedroom/study and to the formal dining room. The kitchen is completely open to the great room and features a stylish snack-bar island and a bay window in the breakfast nook. The master suite offers a tray ceiling and a skylit bath. Two secondary bedrooms share a full bath on the opposite side of the house. Bonus space over the garage may be developed in the future.

SQUARE FOOTAGE:
1,832
BONUS SPACE:
425 sq. ft.
BEDROOMS:
3
BATHROOMS:
2
WIDTH:
65' - 4"
DEPTH:
62' - 0"

Order online at eplans.com

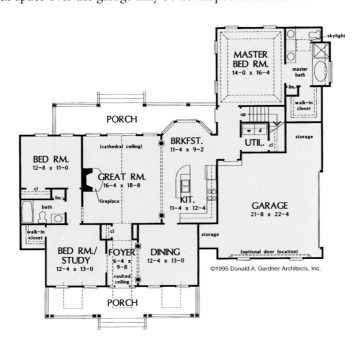

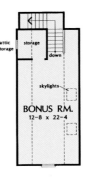

©1995 Donald A. Gardner Architects, Inc.

PLAN:
HPK3300066

SQUARE FOOTAGE:
1,632

BEDROOMS:
3

BATHROOMS:
2

WIDTH:
62' - 4"

DEPTH:
55' - 2"

Order online at eplans.com

This country home has a big heart in a cozy package. Special touches—interior columns, a bay window, and dormers—add elegance. The central great room features a cathedral ceiling and a fireplace. A clerestory window splashes the room with natural light. The open kitchen easily services the breakfast area and the nearby dining room. The private master bedroom, with a tray ceiling and a walk-in closet, boasts amenities found in much larger homes. The bath features a skylight and a whirlpool tub. Two additional bedrooms share a bath. The front bedroom includes a walk-in closet and would make a nice study with an optional foyer entrance.

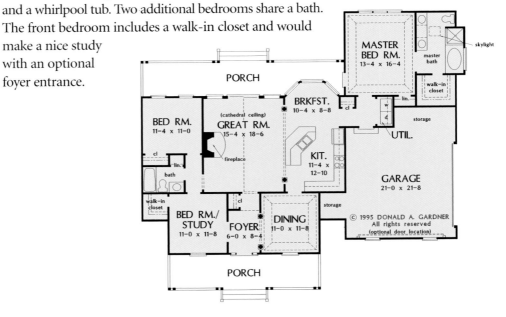

PLAN:
HPK3300067

Dormers, arched windows, and covered porches lend this home its country appeal. Inside, the foyer opens to the dining room on the right and leads through a columned entrance to the great room. The open kitchen easily serves the great room, the breakfast area, and the dining room. A cathedral ceiling graces the master suite, which is complete with a walk-in closet and a private bath. Two family bedrooms share a hall bath.

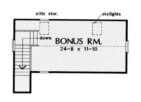

SQUARE FOOTAGE:
1,815
BONUS SPACE:
336 sq. ft.
BEDROOMS:
3
BATHROOMS:
2
WIDTH:
70' - 8"
DEPTH:
70' - 2"

Order online at eplans.com

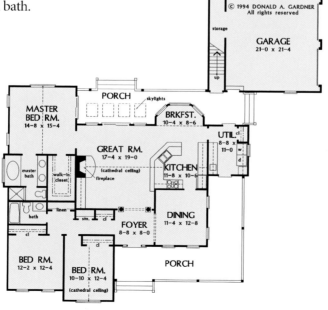

© 2005 Donald A. Gardner, Inc.

PLAN:

HPK3300068

SQUARE FOOTAGE:
1,965

BEDROOMS:
4

BATHROOMS:
2

WIDTH:
74' - 4"

DEPTH:
56' - 6"

Order online at eplans.com

Designed with a touch of farmhouse flair, this home combines a modern floor plan with the look of yesterday. The stunning exterior is made up of columns, several dormer windows, and porches that wrap almost entirely around the home. Inside, bay windows expand the versatile study/bedroom, dining room, and master bedroom. Each crowned with a tray ceiling, these rooms are nothing short of luxurious. The master bedroom also features a barrel vault, and the master bath includes a separate tub and shower with built-in seat. The breakfast room and kitchen are open to the great room and create a natural traffic flow between the rooms. A spacious rear porch completes the home and provides ample space for outdoor entertaining.

Rear Exterior

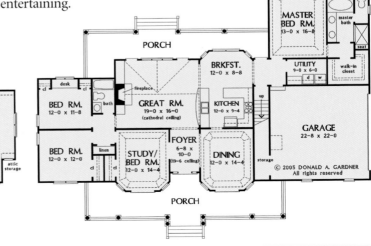

ORDER BLUEPRINTS 24 HOURS, 7 DAYS A WEEK, AT 1-800-521-6797 OR EPLANS.COM

PLAN:
HPK3300069

SQUARE FOOTAGE:
1,576

BEDROOMS:
3

BATHROOMS:
2

WIDTH:
60' - 6"

DEPTH:
47' - 3"

Order online at eplans.com

© 1993 Donald A. Gardner Architects, Inc.

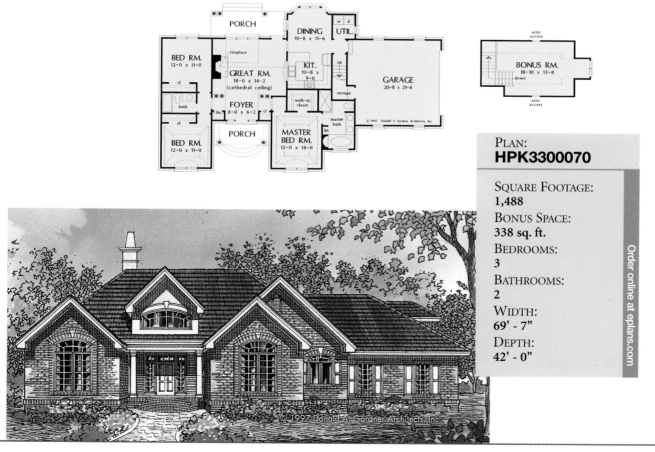

PLAN:
HPK3300070

SQUARE FOOTAGE:
1,488

BONUS SPACE:
338 sq. ft.

BEDROOMS:
3

BATHROOMS:
2

WIDTH:
69' - 7"

DEPTH:
42' - 0"

Order online at eplans.com

© 1992 Donald A. Gardner Architects, Inc.

S. MATTHEWS

PLAN:

HPK3300071

SQUARE FOOTAGE:
1,287
BEDROOMS:
3
BATHROOMS:
2
WIDTH:
66' - 4"
DEPTH:
48' - 0"

Order online at eplans.com

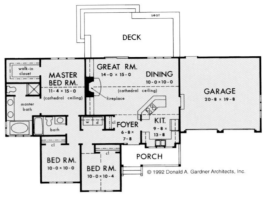

© 1992 Donald A. Gardner Architects, Inc.

PLAN:

HPK3300072

SQUARE FOOTAGE:
1,428
BONUS SPACE:
313 sq. ft.
BEDROOMS:
3
BATHROOMS:
2
WIDTH:
52' - 8"
DEPTH:
52' - 4"

Order online at eplans.com

©1998 Donald A. Gardner, Inc.

© 1995 Donald A. Gardner Architects, Inc.   S. NATHAN

PLAN:
HPK3300073

SQUARE FOOTAGE:
1,633
BONUS SPACE:
595 sq. ft.
BEDROOMS:
3
BATHROOMS:
2
WIDTH:
65' - 4"
DEPTH:
55' - 4"

Stylish rooms and comfortable arrangements make this country home unique and inviting. The foyer opens from a quaint covered porch and leads to the expansive great room, which boasts a cathedral ceiling, an extended-hearth fireplace, and access to the rear deck. The kitchen serves the formal dining room as well as the bayed breakfast nook, which offers windows that bring in the outdoors. A secluded master suite nestles to the rear of the plan and features a U-shaped walk-in closet, a garden tub, and twin vanities. Two nearby bedrooms—or make one a study—share a full bath and a gallery hall that leads back to the foyer.

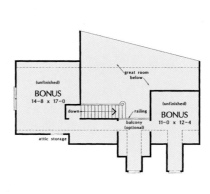

© 1994 Donald A. Gardner Architects, Inc.

PLAN:
HPK3300074

SQUARE FOOTAGE:
1,807
BONUS SPACE:
419 sq. ft.
BEDROOMS:
3
BATHROOMS:
2
WIDTH:
70' - 8"
DEPTH:
52' - 8"

Order online at eplans.com

This comfortable country home begins with a front porch that opens to a columned foyer. To the right, enter the formal dining room. Decorative columns define the central great room, which boasts wide views of the outdoors. A breakfast nook nearby accommodates casual dining. The master suite and the great room open to the rear porch. Family bedrooms share a full bath with dual lavatories.

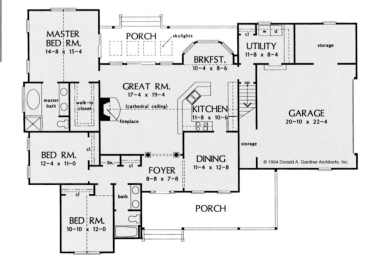

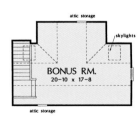

© 1997 Donald A. Gardner Architects, Inc.

A classic country exterior enriches the appearance of this economical home. A grand front porch and two skylit back porches encourage weekend relaxation. The great room features a cathedral ceiling and a fireplace with adjacent built-ins. The master suite offers a double-door entry, back-porch access, and a tray ceiling. The master bath has a garden tub set in the corner, a separate shower, twin vanities, and a skylight. Loads of storage, an open floor plan, and walls of windows make this three-bedroom plan very livable.

PLAN:
HPK3300075

SQUARE FOOTAGE:
1,652

BONUS SPACE:
367 sq. ft.

BEDROOMS:
3

BATHROOMS:
2

WIDTH:
64' - 4"

DEPTH:
51' - 0"

Order online at eplans.com

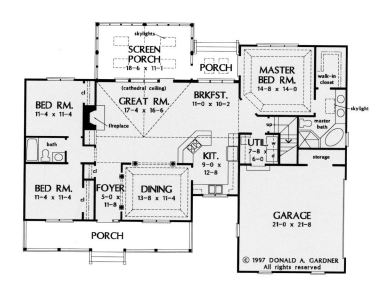

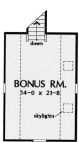

PLAN:

HPK3300076

SQUARE FOOTAGE:
1,954

BEDROOMS:
3

BATHROOMS:
2 ½

WIDTH:
71' - 3"

DEPTH:
62' - 6"

Order online at eplans.com

This beautiful brick country home has all the amenities needed for today's active family. Covered front and back porches, along with a rear deck, provide plenty of room for outdoor enjoyment. Inside, focus is on the large great room with its cathedral ceiling and welcoming fireplace. To the right, columns separate the kitchen and breakfast area from the great room without enclosing them. Chefs of all ages will appreciate the convenience of the kitchen with its center island and additional eating space. The master bedroom provides a splendid private retreat, featuring a cathedral ceiling and large walk-in closet. The luxurious master bath shares a double-bowl vanity, a separate shower, and a relaxing skylit whirlpool tub. At the opposite end of the plan, two additional bedrooms share a full bath. A skylit bonus room above the garage allows for additional living space.

Rear Exterior

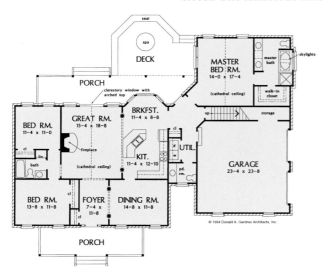

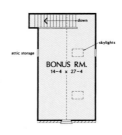

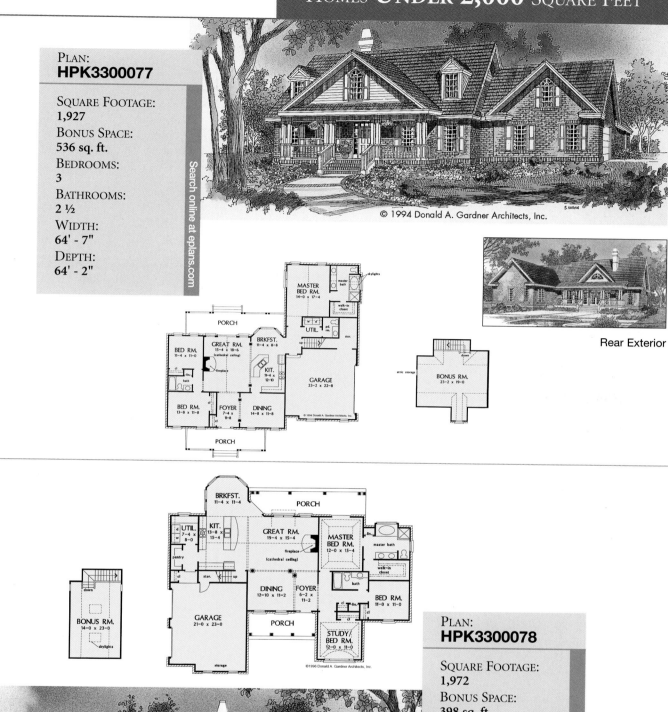

PLAN:
HPK3300077

SQUARE FOOTAGE:
1,927

BONUS SPACE:
536 sq. ft.

BEDROOMS:
3

BATHROOMS:
2 ½

WIDTH:
64' - 7"

DEPTH:
64' - 2"

Search online at eplans.com

© 1994 Donald A. Gardner Architects, Inc.

Rear Exterior

PLAN:
HPK3300078

SQUARE FOOTAGE:
1,972

BONUS SPACE:
398 sq. ft.

BEDROOMS:
3

BATHROOMS:
2

WIDTH:
67' - 7"

DEPTH:
56' - 7"

Order online at eplans.com

© 1996 Donald A. Gardner Architects, Inc.

PLAN:
HPK3300079

SQUARE FOOTAGE:
1,932

BEDROOMS:
4

BATHROOMS:
3

WIDTH:
63' - 0"

DEPTH:
45' - 0"

FOUNDATION:
Crawlspace, Unfinished Walkout Basement

Order online at eplans.com

Special architectural aspects turn this quaint home into much more than just another one-story ranch design. A central great room acts as the hub of the plan and is graced by a fireplace flanked on either side by windows. It is separated from the kitchen by a convenient serving bar. Formal dining is accomplished toward the front of the plan in a room with a tray ceiling. Casual dining takes place in the breakfast room with its full wall of glass. Two bedrooms to the left share a full bath. The master suite and one additional bedroom are to the right.

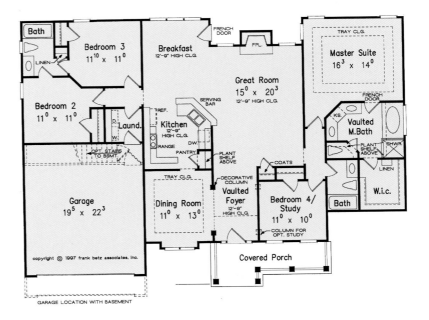

PLAN:

HPK3300080

Gentle arched lintels harmonize with the high hipped roof to create an elevation that is both welcoming and elegant. This efficient plan minimizes hallway space in order to maximize useable living areas. A favorite feature of this home is the "elbow-bend" galley kitchen that has easy access to the dining room and breakfast room—plus a full-length serving bar open to the great room. The master suite has a cozy sitting room and a compartmented bath. Two family bedrooms share a full hall bath.

SQUARE FOOTAGE:
1,575
BEDROOMS:
3
BATHROOMS:
2
WIDTH:
50' - 0"
DEPTH:
52' - 6"
FOUNDATION:
Crawlspace, Unfinished Walkout Basement

Order online at eplans.com

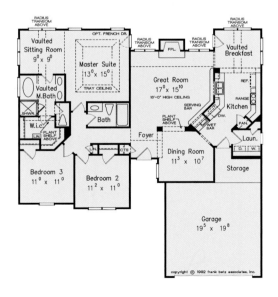

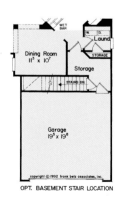

OPT. BASEMENT STAIR LOCATION

PLAN:
HPK3300081

SQUARE FOOTAGE:
1,232

BEDROOMS:
3

BATHROOMS:
2

WIDTH:
46' - 0"

DEPTH:
44' - 4"

FOUNDATION:
Crawlspace, Slab, Unfinished Walkout Basement

Order online at eplans.com

Gabled rooflines, shutters, and siding—all elements of a fine facade. The foyer opens directly to the vaulted great room, where a fireplace waits to warm cool winter evenings. Nearby, the efficient kitchen easily accesses the dining room. Two secondary bedrooms share a full hall bath. The deluxe master suite offers a vaulted bath and a spacious walk-in closet. A laundry room is located in between the master suite and the two-car garage.

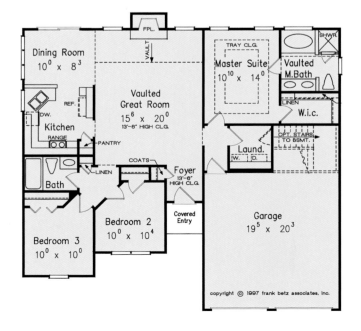

PLAN:
HPK3300082

SQUARE FOOTAGE:
1,373
BEDROOMS:
3
BATHROOMS:
2
WIDTH:
50' - 4"
DEPTH:
45' - 0"
FOUNDATION:
Crawlspace, Unfinished Walkout Basement

Order online at eplans.com

A steep gabled roofline punctuated with dormer windows and a columned front porch give a traditional welcome to this family home. A vaulted ceiling tops the family and dining rooms, which are nicely accented with a fireplace and bright windows. An amenity-filled kitchen opens to the breakfast room. The master suite has a refined tray ceiling and a vaulted bath. Two family bedrooms, a laundry center, and a full bath—with private access from Bedroom 3—complete this stylish plan.

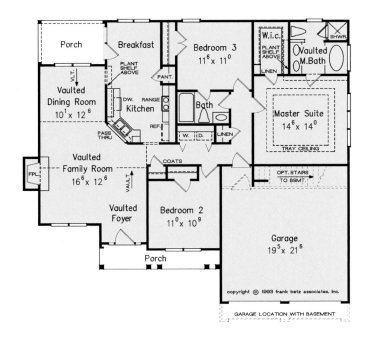

PLAN:
HPK3300083

SQUARE FOOTAGE:
1,671

BEDROOMS:
3

BATHROOMS:
2

WIDTH:
50' - 0"

DEPTH:
51' - 0"

FOUNDATION:
Crawlspace, Slab, Unfinished Walkout Basement

Order online at eplans.com

A symmetrical gables, a columned porch, and an abundance of windows brighten the exterior of this compact home. An efficient kitchen boasts a pantry and a serving bar that it shares with the formal dining room and the vaulted family room. A sunny breakfast room and nearby laundry room complete the living zone. Be sure to notice extras such as the focal-point fireplace in the family room and a plant shelf in the laundry room. The sumptuous master suite offers a door to the backyard, a vaulted sitting area, and a pampering bath. Two family bedrooms share a hall bath.

PLAN:

HPK3300084

This cozy country cottage is enhanced with a front-facing planter box above the garage and a charming covered porch. The foyer leads to a vaulted great room, complete with a fireplace and radius windows. Decorative columns complement the entrance to the dining room, as does the arched opening. The master suite resides on the left side of the plan, resplendent with a vaulted sitting room, tray ceiling, and French doors to the vaulted full bath. On the right side, two additional bedrooms share a full hall bath.

SQUARE FOOTAGE:
1,749
BONUS SPACE:
308 sq. ft.
BEDROOMS:
3
BATHROOMS:
2
WIDTH:
54' - 0"
DEPTH:
56' - 6"
FOUNDATION:
Crawlspace, Slab, Unfinished Walkout Basement

Order online at eplans.com

OPTIONAL BONUS ROOM PLAN

GARAGE LOCATION W/ BASEMENT

Rear Exterior

PLAN:
HPK3300085

SQUARE FOOTAGE:
1,875

BEDROOMS:
3

BATHROOMS:
2

WIDTH:
56' - 0"

DEPTH:
50' - 6"

FOUNDATION:
Crawlspace, Slab, Unfinished Walkout Basement

Order online at eplans.com

An oversized muntin window gives a cheerful first impression to this well-appointed family home. Boxed columns frame the formal dining room to one side of the foyer; the living room or den is to the other side. A vaulted ceiling soars over the family room. A lovely fireplace, flanked by windows, and a wraparound serving bar make this room the heart of family gatherings. The kitchen has all the amenities, including a sunny breakfast nook. The master suite is split from the two family bedrooms and features a lush compartmented bath and walk-in closet. Two family bedrooms, a hall bath, and a laundry room complete this favorite plan.

© Stephen Fuller, Inc.

Delightfully different, this brick one-story home has everything for the active family. The foyer opens to a formal dining room, accented with four columns, and a great room with a fireplace and French doors to the rear deck. The efficient kitchen has an attached light-filled breakfast nook. The master bath features a tray ceiling, His and Hers walk-in closets, a double-sink vanity, and a garden tub. Access the two-car garage through the laundry room.

PLAN:
HPK3300086

SQUARE FOOTAGE:
1,733
BEDROOMS:
3
BATHROOMS:
2 ½
WIDTH:
55' - 6"
DEPTH:
57' - 6"
FOUNDATION:
Finished Walkout Basement

Order online at eplans.com

PLAN:
HPK3300087

SQUARE FOOTAGE:
1,580

BEDROOMS:
3

BATHROOMS:
2

WIDTH:
50' - 0"

DEPTH:
44' - 0"

FOUNDATION:
Slab

Order online at eplans.com

A super-efficient layout combined with attractive exterior elements make this an outstanding starter home. The galley-style kitchen pairs with a breakfast area that is large enough for several people to comfortably keep the cook company. Two family bedrooms flank the dining room. The master suite is buffered by the grand room and offers twin walk-in closets and a private full bath.

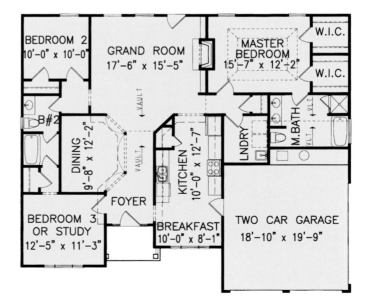

PLAN:
HPK3300088

SQUARE FOOTAGE:	1,656
BONUS SPACE:	368 sq. ft.
BEDROOMS:	3
BATHROOMS:	2
WIDTH:	50' - 0"
DEPTH:	48' - 0"
FOUNDATION:	Slab

Order online at eplans.com

Small Arts and Crafts details enhance this ranch-style home. Designed using open space and natural traffic flow for an unobstructed layout, it includes split bedrooms, an efficient yet spacious kitchen with bumped-out breakfast nook, and a dining room oriented to take advantage of the corner fireplace in the grand room. The master suite introduces itself with double doors and features a private bath and walk-in closet.

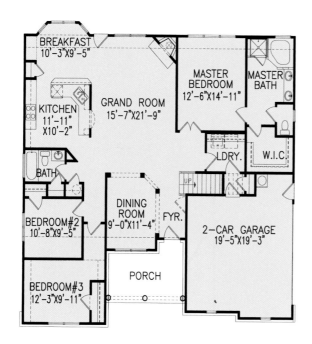

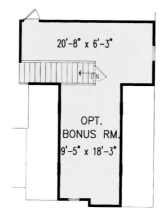

PLAN:
HPK3300089

SQUARE FOOTAGE:
1,821

BONUS SPACE:
191 sq. ft.

BEDROOMS:
3

BATHROOMS:
2

WIDTH:
54' - 0"

DEPTH:
54' - 0"

FOUNDATION:
Slab

Order online at eplans.com

This eye-pleasing beauty, with its clerestory window and front columns, has an interior uniquely designed for enjoyment and comfort. Enter the foyer from a covered front stoop. The dining room is to the right, very elegant with an octagonal ceiling. Straight ahead, the main living room features a warming fireplace and vaulted ceiling. The roomy kitchen opens to a sunlit breakfast alcove. On the left side of the plan, the master suite embraces a huge walk-in closet and sumptuous bath with a double-sink vanity. To the right, two more bedrooms share a bath and are conveniently located near the laundry room. Over the two-car garage, additional space is available to be used as you want.

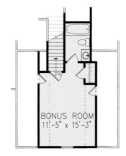

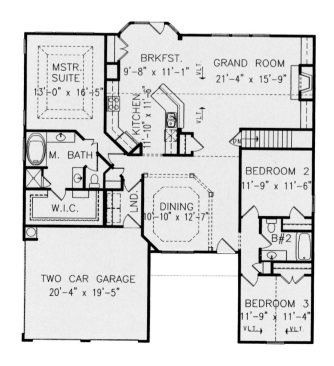

Brick with a hint of siding, keystone lintels, and window shutters complement this home's exterior. To the right of the foyer, find two family bedrooms and a hall bath. To the left, the dining room features a decorative ceiling and defining columns. The grand room, with built-ins and a fireplace, shares a breakfast space and the open kitchen. A private hall leads to the master suite. Full bath amenities and a walk-in closet complete this space.

PLAN:
HPK3300090

SQUARE FOOTAGE:
1,923
BEDROOMS:
3
BATHROOMS:
2
WIDTH:
48' - 0"
DEPTH:
53' - 0"
FOUNDATION:
Unfinished Walkout Basement

Order online at eplans.com

PLAN:

HPK3300091

SQUARE FOOTAGE:
1,985

BONUS SPACE:
191 sq. ft.

BEDROOMS:
3

BATHROOMS:
2

WIDTH:
54' - 0"

DEPTH:
54' - 0"

FOUNDATION:
Slab

Order online at eplans.com

Gracious living starts with a balanced and appealing facade. Enjoy the open pediment above the covered porch and the shutters framing the front windows. A formal dining room offers the right amount of space for get-togethers. The family room does double duty for guests and casual time. An adjoining sunroom is a perfect spot to close the evening or start the day. Breakfast will be bright with natural light from the bay just off the kitchen. Two bedrooms, split from the master, are secluded to the right of the plan and share a full bath. A large walk-in closet and private bath outfit the master suite.

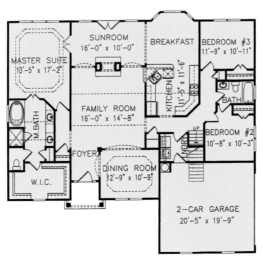

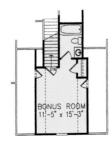

PLAN:

HPK3300092

SQUARE FOOTAGE:
1,458

BONUS SPACE:
256 sq. ft.

BEDROOMS:
3

BATHROOMS:
2

WIDTH:
47' - 7"

DEPTH:
46' - 5"

FOUNDATION:
Slab

Order online at eplans.com

© 2002 BuildinGraphics Architecture used by permission by Living Concepts

PLAN:

HPK3300093

SQUARE FOOTAGE:
1,537

BEDROOMS:
3

BATHROOMS:
2

WIDTH:
59' - 8"

DEPTH:
42' - 2"

FOUNDATION:
Unfinished Basement

Order online at eplans.com

PLAN:
HPK3300094

SQUARE FOOTAGE:
1,598

BEDROOMS:
3

BATHROOMS:
2

WIDTH:
59' - 4"

DEPTH:
45' - 6"

FOUNDATION:
Unfinished Basement

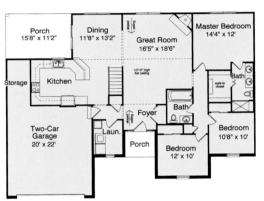

PLAN:
HPK3300095

SQUARE FOOTAGE:
1,759

BEDROOMS:
3

BATHROOMS:
2

WIDTH:
82' - 10"

DEPTH:
47' - 5"

FOUNDATION:
Unfinished Basement

ORDER BLUEPRINTS 24 HOURS, 7 DAYS A WEEK, AT 1-800-521-6797 OR EPLANS.COM

PLAN:

HPK3300096

SQUARE FOOTAGE:
1,860
BEDROOMS:
3
BATHROOMS:
2
WIDTH:
85' - 4"
DEPTH:
36' - 8"
FOUNDATION:
Unfinished Basement

Order online at eplans.com

Traditional symmetry graces the facade of this charming brick home. The covered entry announces the foyer, which opens to the great room with a vaulted ceiling and corner fireplace. To the right of the foyer is the spacious living/dining room. The island kitchen, with its convenient snack bar, is situated between the dining room and the sunny breakfast bay. Access to the rear porch and the garage as well as the utility room is found just to the right of this area. The left wing holds the master suite, two family bedrooms, and a shared full bath.

PLAN:

HPK3300097

SQUARE FOOTAGE:
1,442

BEDROOMS:
3

BATHROOMS:
2

WIDTH:
52' - 8"

DEPTH:
45' - 0"

FOUNDATION:
Unfinished Walkout Basement

Order online at eplans.com

This delightful home offers space-saving convenience and functional living space. The dining area and living room combine to create a great room that is decorated by a gas fireplace and 11-foot ceiling height. The fully equipped kitchen offers a counter with seating, a dishwasher, and a built-in microwave. Split bedrooms offer privacy to the master suite, which features a 9-foot-tall ceiling, double bowl vanity, and compartmented bath. A walk-in closet in the master and one at the garage entry offer great storage. A full basement with access to the rear yard offers the option to expand the square footage of this charming home.

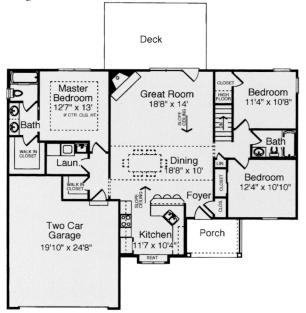

ORDER BLUEPRINTS 24 HOURS, 7 DAYS A WEEK, AT 1-800-521-6797 OR EPLANS.COM

PLAN:
HPK3300098

Designed to provide private spaces for each household member, this three-bedroom ranch home offers a stylish exterior with brick, stone, cedar shakes, and an inviting covered porch. The interior features a spacious great room, U-shaped kitchen with counter seating, and adjacent dining area. The ceiling throughout this space slopes to 13 feet, adding a dramatic effect. The master bedroom suite offers a private bath with double bowl vanity, and the walk-out basement shows a potential rec room with wet bar, a fourth bedroom, and a third bath.

SQUARE FOOTAGE:
1,483
BEDROOMS:
3
BATHROOMS:
2
WIDTH:
70' - 2"
DEPTH:
50' - 8"
FOUNDATION:
Finished Walkout Basement

Order online at eplans.com

PLAN:
HPK3300099

SQUARE FOOTAGE:
1,498

BEDROOMS:
3

BATHROOMS:
2

WIDTH:
66' - 4"

DEPTH:
44' - 10"

FOUNDATION:
Unfinished Basement

PLAN:
HPK3300100

SQUARE FOOTAGE:
1,563

BEDROOMS:
3

BATHROOMS:
2

WIDTH:
69' - 4"

DEPTH:
42' - 4"

FOUNDATION:
Unfinished Basement

PLAN:
HPK3300101

SQUARE FOOTAGE:
1,593
BEDROOMS:
3
BATHROOMS:
2
WIDTH:
60' - 0"
DEPTH:
48' - 10"
FOUNDATION:
Unfinished Basement

Order online at eplans.com

Multiple gables, a transom over the entry door, and a brick-and-stone exterior combine to create an exciting front to this beautiful one-story home. The open foyer offers a view through the great room to the rear yard. A dramatic fireplace and sloped ceiling decorate the fashionable great room. The spacious kitchen and breakfast room feature a favorable indoor/outdoor relationship. The first-floor master bedroom, with a tray ceiling, private bath, and extra-large walk-in closet, pampers homeowners with its size and luxury. Two additional bedrooms complete this spectacular home.

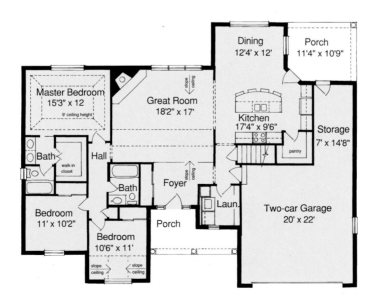

PLAN:
HPK3300102

SQUARE FOOTAGE:
1,611

BEDROOMS:
3

BATHROOMS:
2

WIDTH:
66' - 4"

DEPTH:
43' - 10"

FOUNDATION:
Unfinished Basement

Order online at eplans.com

PLAN:
HPK3300103

SQUARE FOOTAGE:
1,824

BEDROOMS:
3

BATHROOMS:
2

WIDTH:
74' - 0"

DEPTH:
52' - 10"

FOUNDATION:
Unfinished Basement

Order online at eplans.com

PLAN:

HPK3300002

SQUARE FOOTAGE:
1,751

BEDROOMS:
3

BATHROOMS:
2

WIDTH:
72' - 6"

DEPTH:
42' - 3"

FOUNDATION:
Unfinished Basement

Order online at eplans.com

Exciting ceiling treatments and an open floor plan create spaciousness in this lovely three-bedroom home. The foyer, dining room, and master bedroom all have 9-foot ceilings; in the great room, a dramatic sloped ceiling soars to 12 feet. A covered porch greets guests, and a second porch, off the breakfast area, visually expands the home and enhances outdoor enjoyment. The master suite offers comfort and luxury, with a whirlpool tub, shower, and double vanity. A full basement can be finished at a later date as your family grows.

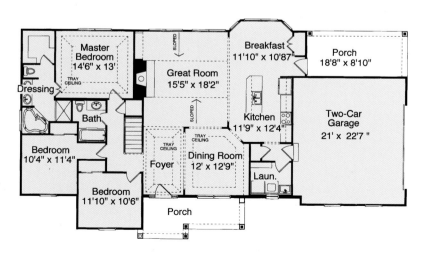

PLAN:
HPK3300104

SQUARE FOOTAGE:
1,623

BEDROOMS:
3

BATHROOMS:
2

WIDTH:
75' - 0"

DEPTH:
39' - 1"

FOUNDATION:
Unfinished Basement

Order online at eplans.com

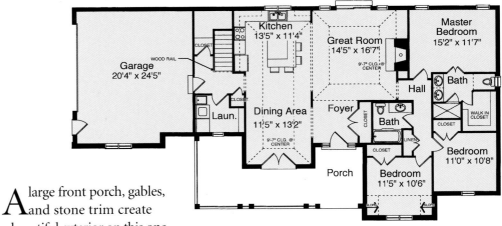

A large front porch, gables, and stone trim create a beautiful exterior on this one-level home. Interior spaces comprise vaulted ceilings, an open floor plan, and a great view to the rear yard. The kitchen features an island with seating and, combined with the dining area, becomes a large gathering space. Ample closets create great storage areas, and the master bedroom offers a private bath with a dual bowl-vanity, shower, and spacious walk-in closet. A full basement can expand this home to double its original size.

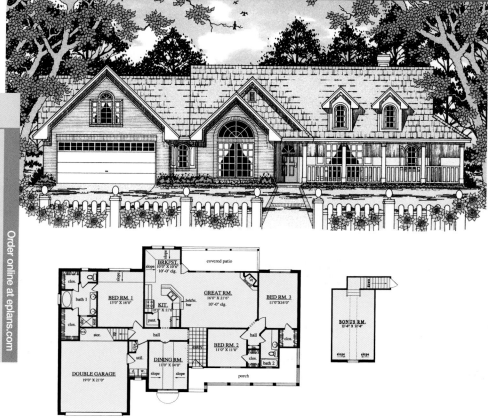

PLAN:
HPK3300105

SQUARE FOOTAGE:
1,880

BONUS SPACE:
328 sq. ft.

BEDROOMS:
3

BATHROOMS:
2

WIDTH:
68' - 6"

DEPTH:
49' - 0"

FOUNDATION:
Crawlspace, Slab

Order online at eplans.com

PLAN:
HPK3300106

SQUARE FOOTAGE:
1,484

BEDROOMS:
3

BATHROOMS:
2

WIDTH:
52' - 10"

DEPTH:
50' - 6"

FOUNDATION:
Crawlspace, Slab

Order online at eplans.com

PLAN:
HPK3300107

SQUARE FOOTAGE:
1,253
BEDROOMS:
3
BATHROOMS:
2
WIDTH:
44' - 0"
DEPTH:
34' - 0"
FOUNDATION:
Crawlspace, Slab

PLAN:
HPK3300004

SQUARE FOOTAGE:
1,667
BEDROOMS:
3
BATHROOMS:
2
WIDTH:
70' - 0"
DEPTH:
34' - 4"
FOUNDATION:
Crawlspace, Slab, Unfinished Basement

Contemporary with a country twist, this modern ranch home has it all. Two verandas and a screened porch enlarge the plan and enhance indoor/outdoor livability. The sloped ceiling in the gathering room gives this area an open, airy quality. The breakfast room, with its wealth of windows, will be a cheerful and bright space to enjoy a cup of morning coffee. Added extras provide a thoughtful touch: abundant storage space, walk-in pantry, built-in planning desk, and pass-through snack bar. The master suite features a pampering whirlpool tub to soak your cares away.

PLAN:
HPK3300109

SQUARE FOOTAGE:
1,951
BEDROOMS:
3
BATHROOMS:
2
WIDTH:
56' - 0"
DEPTH:
48' - 8"
FOUNDATION:
Unfinished Basement

Order online at eplans.com

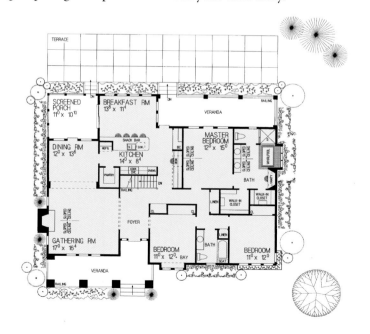

Courtesy of Home Planners. This home, as shown in the photography, may differ from

PLAN:

HPK3300110

SQUARE FOOTAGE:
1,530

BEDROOMS:
3

BATHROOMS:
2

WIDTH:
51' - 4"

DEPTH:
55' - 6"

FOUNDATION:
Unfinished Basement

Order online at eplans.com

This charming one-story traditional design offers plenty of livability in a compact size. Thoughtful zoning puts all sleeping areas to one side of the house, away from household activity in the living and service areas. The home includes a spacious gathering room with a sloped ceiling in addition to a formal dining room and a separate breakfast room. There's also a handy pass-through between the breakfast room and the large, efficient kitchen. The laundry room is strategically located adjacent to the garage and the breakfast/kitchen area for easy access. The master bedroom comprises a private bath and a walk-in closet. A third bedroom, just off the foyer, can double as a sizable study.

PLAN:
HPK3300111

This charming one-story traditional home greets visitors with a covered porch. A uniquely shaped galley-style kitchen shares a snack bar with the spacious gathering room, where a fireplace is the focal point. The dining room features sliding glass doors to the rear terrace, as does the master bedroom. This bedroom area also includes a luxury bath with a whirlpool tub and separate dressing room. Two additional bedrooms, one that could double as a study, are located at the front of the home. The two-car garage features a large storage area and can be reached through the service entrance or from the rear terrace.

SQUARE FOOTAGE:
1,830
BEDROOMS:
3
BATHROOMS:
2
WIDTH:
75' - 0"
DEPTH:
43' - 5"
FOUNDATION:
Unfinished Basement

Order online at eplans.com

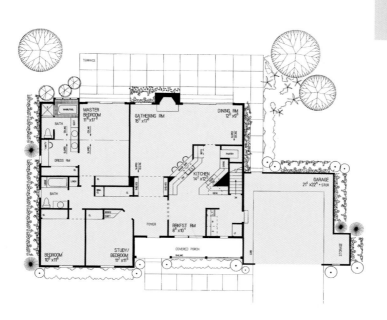

PLAN:
HPK3300112

SQUARE FOOTAGE:
1,515
BEDROOMS:
3
BATHROOMS:
2
WIDTH:
71' - 8"
DEPTH:
36' - 0"
FOUNDATION:
Unfinished Basement

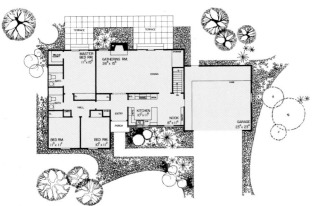

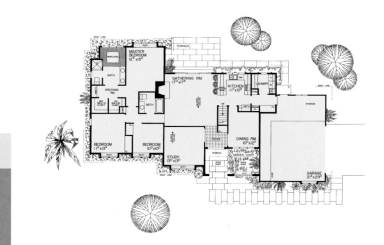

PLAN:
HPK3300113

SQUARE FOOTAGE:
1,913
BEDROOMS:
3
BATHROOMS:
2
WIDTH:
77' - 10"
DEPTH:
46' - 4"
FOUNDATION:
Unfinished Basement

This charming ranch-style home is perfect for empty-nesters or a small family. A study of the floor plan reveals fine livability. There are two full baths, a family room, an efficient work center, a formal dining area, bulk storage facilities, and sliding glass doors to the quiet and living terraces. The laundry room is strategically located near the kitchen. Three bedrooms include a master bedroom with double closets and a full private bath. Two secondary bedrooms share a full hall bath.

PLAN:
HPK3300114

SQUARE FOOTAGE:
1,344
BEDROOMS:
3
BATHROOMS:
2
WIDTH:
68' - 0"
DEPTH:
28' - 0"
FOUNDATION:
Crawlspace

Order online at eplans.com

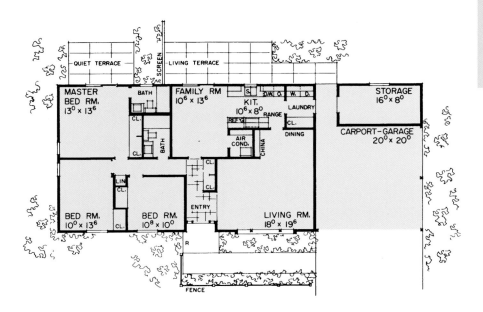

PLAN:

HPK3300115

SQUARE FOOTAGE:
1,937

BONUS SPACE:
414 sq. ft.

BEDROOMS:
3

BATHROOMS:
2

WIDTH:
62' - 8"

DEPTH:
56' - 0"

FOUNDATION:
Crawlspace

Order online at eplans.com

Country living in a unique floor plan makes this design the perfect choice for a family. The covered front porch opens to an angled foyer that leads to a large great room with a sloped ceiling and fireplace. To the right is the formal dining room, defined by columns and with plenty of windows overlooking the porch. Two secondary bedrooms share a full bath at the front of the plan. Connected to the two-car garage via the laundry room, the kitchen provides an island cooktop and a quaint morning room. The master suite offers a retreat with a sloped ceiling, walk-in closet, and bath with a whirlpool tub.

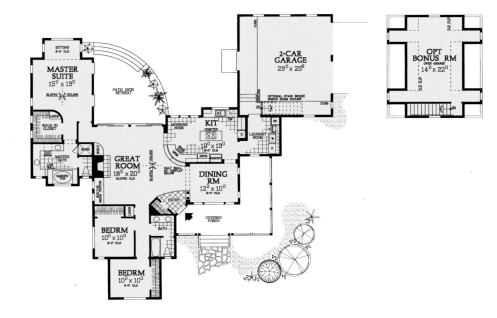

PLAN:
HPK3300116

SQUARE FOOTAGE:
1,541

BEDROOMS:
3

BATHROOMS:
2

WIDTH:
87' - 0"

DEPTH:
44' - 0"

FOUNDATION:
Crawlspace, Unfinished Basement

This popular design begins with a wraparound covered porch made even more charming with turned-wood spindles. The entry opens directly to the great room, which is warmed by a woodstove. The adjoining dining room offers access to a screened porch for outdoor after-dinner leisure. A country kitchen features a center island and a breakfast bay for casual meals. Family bedrooms share a full bath with a soaking tub. The two-car garage connects to the plan via the screened porch.

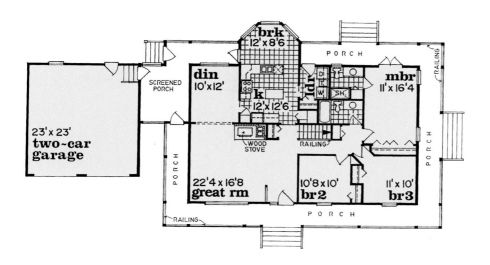

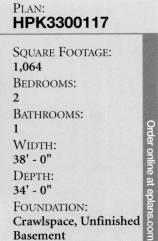

PLAN:
HPK3300117

SQUARE FOOTAGE:
1,064

BEDROOMS:
2

BATHROOMS:
1

WIDTH:
38' - 0"

DEPTH:
34' - 0"

FOUNDATION:
Crawlspace, Unfinished Basement

Order online at eplans.com

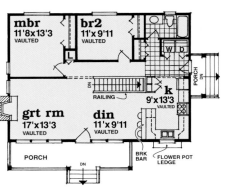

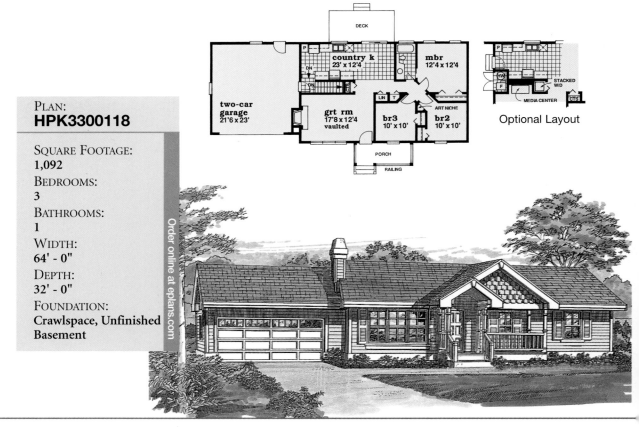

Optional Layout

PLAN:
HPK3300118

SQUARE FOOTAGE:
1,092

BEDROOMS:
3

BATHROOMS:
1

WIDTH:
64' - 0"

DEPTH:
32' - 0"

FOUNDATION:
Crawlspace, Unfinished Basement

Order online at eplans.com

PLAN:
HPK3300119

SQUARE FOOTAGE:
1,392
BEDROOMS:
3
BATHROOMS:
2
WIDTH:
44' - 0"
DEPTH:
52' - 6"
FOUNDATION:
Crawlspace, Unfinished Basement

Order online at eplans.com

Traditional corner columns add prestige to this three-bedroom bungalow. The vaulted living room features a gas fireplace and a built-in media center. An open kitchen with a work island adjoins the dining room that contains a large bay window and double French doors to the rear deck. Natural light from the skylights in the main hallways creates a dramatic effect. The master suite is appointed with His and Hers wall closets and a private bath. Family bedrooms share a full hall bath. The laundry room has space for a full-sized washer and dryer with cabinets overhead. The crawlspace option allows for a convenient homework space between the dining room and living room.

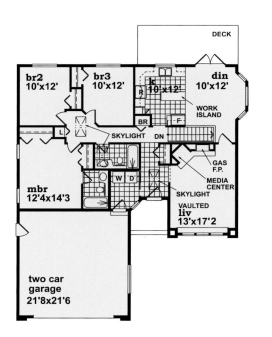

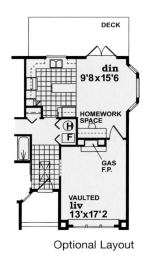

Optional Layout

PLAN:

HPK3300120

SQUARE FOOTAGE:
1,298

BEDROOMS:
3

BATHROOMS:
2

WIDTH:
70' - 0"

DEPTH:
36' - 0"

FOUNDATION:
Crawlspace, Unfinished Basement

Order online at eplans.com

A front veranda, cedar lattice, and a solid-stone chimney enhance the appeal of this one-story, country-style home. The open plan begins with the great room, which includes a fireplace and a plant ledge over the wall that separates the living space from the country kitchen. The U-shaped kitchen provides an island work counter and sliding glass doors to the rear deck and screened porch. The master suite also has a wall closet and a private bath with a window seat.

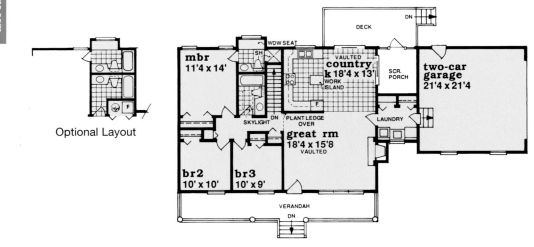

Optional Layout

An eyebrow dormer and a large veranda give guests a warm country greeting outside; inside, vaulted ceilings lend a sense of spaciousness to this three-bedroom home. A bright country kitchen boasts an abundance of counter space and cupboards. The front entry is sheltered by a broad veranda. Built-in amenities adorn the interior, including a pot ledge over the entry coat closet, an art niche, a skylight, and a walk-in pantry and island workstation in the kitchen. A box-bay window and a spa-style tub highlight the master suite. The two-car garage provides a workshop area.

PLAN:
HPK3300121

SQUARE FOOTAGE:
1,408
BEDROOMS:
3
BATHROOMS:
2
WIDTH:
70' - 0"
DEPTH:
34' - 0"
FOUNDATION:
Crawlspace, Unfinished Basement

Order online at eplans.com

Optional Layout

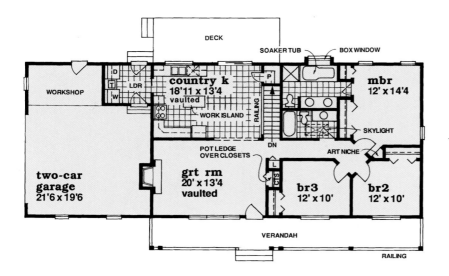

PLAN:
HPK3300122

SQUARE FOOTAGE:
1,578

BEDROOMS:
3

BATHROOMS:
2

WIDTH:
83' - 0"

DEPTH:
40' - 6"

FOUNDATION:
Crawlspace, Unfinished Basement

Order online at eplans.com

With a graceful pediment above and a sturdy, columned veranda below, this quaint home was made for country living. The veranda wraps slightly around on two sides of the facade and permits access to a central foyer with a den (or third bedroom) on the right and the country kitchen on the left. Look for an island work space in the kitchen and a plant ledge over the entry between the great room and the kitchen. A fireplace warms the great room and is flanked by windows overlooking the rear deck. A casually defined dining space has double-door access to this same deck.

PLAN:
HPK3300123

SQUARE FOOTAGE:
1,760
BEDROOMS:
3
BATHROOMS:
2
WIDTH:
68' - 0"
DEPTH:
46' - 0"
FOUNDATION:
Crawlspace, Unfinished Basement

Order online at eplans.com

This brick one-story design offers a covered, railed porch that provides a weather-protected entry to the home. The vaulted foyer carries its ceiling detail into the living room, where there is a fireplace and double-door access to the rear patio. The dining room has a tray ceiling and is located to the right of the entry. A screened porch decorates the breakfast room and allows for protected casual outdoor dining. The kitchen is U-shaped with a center work island and large pantry. A nearby laundry room has access to the two-car garage. Look no further than the master bedroom for true luxury. It boasts a tray ceiling and a full bath with a whirlpool spa, separate shower, and double vanity. Family bedrooms have wall closets and share a full bath.

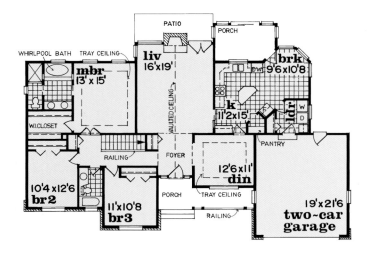

PLAN:
HPK3300124

SQUARE FOOTAGE:
1,398
BEDROOMS:
3
BATHROOMS:
2
WIDTH:
45' - 0"
DEPTH:
50' - 0"
FOUNDATION:
Crawlspace

Order online at eplans.com

PLAN:
HPK3300125

SQUARE FOOTAGE:
1,767
BEDROOMS:
3
BATHROOMS:
2
WIDTH:
48' - 0"
DEPTH:
54' - 6"
FOUNDATION:
Crawlspace

Order online at eplans.com

Slender columns on brick veneer bases immediately catch the eye. Other Craftsman accents on this contemporary home include multipaned windows and textured shake siding filling the apexes of both front gables. The foyer passes a traditional living room and dining room. With a full view of everything going on in the family room, nook, patio, and rear yard, the family chef can converse with people in all of those inner areas from the built-in range. An arched hallway at the juncture of the kitchen and nook leads to the master suite and utility room that connects with the two-car garage. Master suite amenities include a deep walk-in closet, double vanity, walk-in shower, and private toilet. A pass-through in the family room leads to two more bedrooms, where they share use of a central bathroom.

PLAN:
HPK3300126

SQUARE FOOTAGE:
1,884
BEDROOMS:
3
BATHROOMS:
2
WIDTH:
60' - 0"
DEPTH:
50' - 0"
FOUNDATION:
Crawlspace

Order online at eplans.com

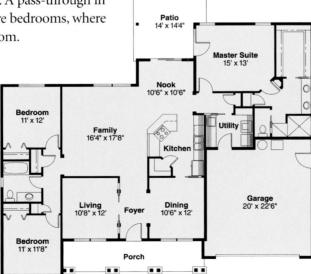

PLAN:
HPK3300127

SQUARE FOOTAGE:
1,876

BEDROOMS:
3

BATHROOMS:
2

WIDTH:
74' - 10"

DEPTH:
56' - 10"

FOUNDATION:
Crawlspace, Slab

Order online at eplans.com

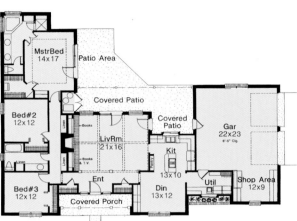

PLAN:
HPK3300003

SQUARE FOOTAGE:
1,902

BEDROOMS:
3

BATHROOMS:
2 ½

WIDTH:
84' - 7"

DEPTH:
34' - 5"

FOUNDATION:
Slab

Order online at eplans.com

A cupola, shutters, arched transoms and an exterior of combined stone and lap siding give this one-story home its country identity. To the left of the entry, the great room's cathedral ceiling and fireplace extend an invitation for family and friends to relax and enjoy themselves. The kitchen and dining room are located nearby. Kitchen amenities include an island cooktop, built-in planning desk, and pantry, while the dining area overlooks and provides access to the covered veranda. A hall leads to sleeping quarters that include two secondary bedrooms and a luxurious master suite.

PLAN:
HPK3300128

SQUARE FOOTAGE:
1,830
BEDROOMS:
3
BATHROOMS:
2
WIDTH:
75' - 0"
DEPTH:
52' - 3"
FOUNDATION:
Crawlspace, Slab

Order online at eplans.com

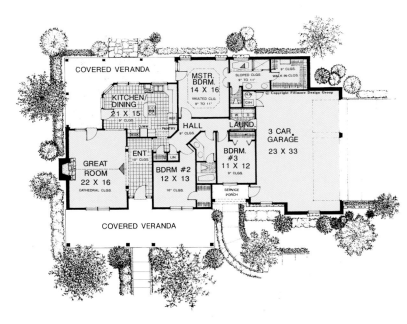

PLAN:
HPK3300129

SQUARE FOOTAGE:
1,899

BEDROOMS:
2

BATHROOMS:
2 ½

WIDTH:
62' - 0"

DEPTH:
68' - 8"

Order online at eplans.com

A hipped dormer on the exterior and a tray ceiling inside highlight the dining room of this traditional Craftsman. Escape to the privacy of the master suite and its own whirlpool tub. The kitchen is tucked away from traffic, but within view of the amply-spaced eating area. The main floor of this house has an additional covered porch in the rear corner leading off of the garage. Both the den and family bedroom feature built-in desks.

DESIGNERS' INK

PLAN:
HPK3300130

SQUARE FOOTAGE:
1,392
BEDROOMS:
3
BATHROOMS:
2
WIDTH:
42' - 0"
DEPTH:
54' - 0"

Order online at eplans.com

With an unusually narrow footprint, this one-story home will fit on most slender lots and still provide a great floor plan. The entry is graced with a handy coat closet and leads back to the spacious great room (note the 10-foot ceiling here) and to the right to two family bedrooms and a full bath. Stairs to the basement level are just beyond the entry hall. The breakfast room and kitchen dominate the left side of the plan. Separating them is a snack-bar counter for quick meals. Pampered amenities in the secluded master bedroom include a walk-in closet, windowed corner whirlpool tub, dual sinks, and a separate shower. A service entrance through the kitchen to the garage leads to a convenient laundry area and broom closet.

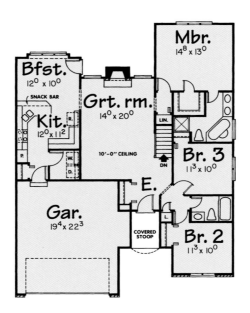

PLAN:
HPK3300131

SQUARE FOOTAGE:
1,478
BEDROOMS:
2
BATHROOMS:
2
WIDTH:
42' - 0"
DEPTH:
55' - 8"

Order online at eplans.com

Ornate brick accents, transom windows, and an arched entry decorate this quaint one-story home. A gallery wall in the entry leads beyond to the great room, where a central fireplace has windows on either side. The breakfast area has a bay window and provides access to the rear covered porch. The master suite offers a walk-in closet, a corner whirlpool tub, and its own door to the covered porch. Opt to convert the den into a third bedroom for extra family or guest space.

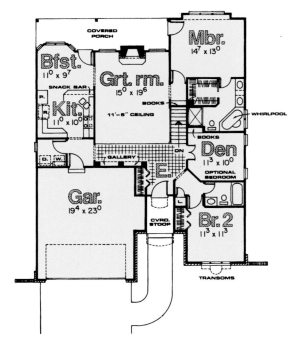

Optional Layout

PLAN:
HPK3300132

SQUARE FOOTAGE:
1,850
BEDROOMS:
3
BATHROOMS:
2
WIDTH:
62' - 0"
DEPTH:
48' - 0"

European style influences the exterior of this distinctive ranch home. Appealing rooflines and a covered porch with repeating arches provide stunning curb appeal. Inside, an impressive 10-foot-high entry greets family and friends. An open concept pervades the kitchen/dinette area. Picture your family enjoying the bayed eating area, wrapping counters, desk, island, and wet bar/servery—ideal for entertaining. The decorative hutch space adds appeal to a formal dining room. Bright windows frame a fireplace in the great room. Sure to please is the service entry to the laundry/mudroom with soaking sink and counter space. Bedroom 2 can easily be converted into a private den. A boxed ceiling decorates the master suite, and three windows provide natural lighting. Dual sinks, a walk-in closet, whirlpool tub, and cedar-lined window seat enhance the master bath.

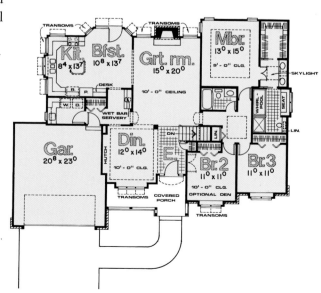

PLAN:

HPK3300133

SQUARE FOOTAGE:
1,001

BEDROOMS:
2

BATHROOMS:
2

WIDTH:
44' - 0"

DEPTH:
38' - 4"

FOUNDATION:
Crawlspace, Slab

PLAN:

HPK3300134

SQUARE FOOTAGE:
1,500

BEDROOMS:
3

BATHROOMS:
2

WIDTH:
61' - 0"

DEPTH:
47' - 4"

FOUNDATION:
Slab

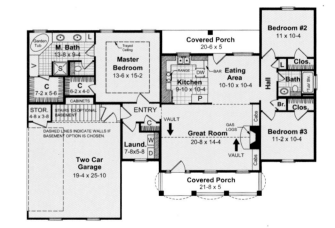

PLAN:
HPK3300135

SQUARE FOOTAGE:
1,433

BEDROOMS:
3

BATHROOMS:
2

WIDTH:
54' - 0"

DEPTH:
41' - 0"

FOUNDATION:
Crawlspace, Slab, Unfinished Basement

Order online at eplans.com

PLAN:
HPK3300136

SQUARE FOOTAGE:
1,698

BEDROOMS:
3

BATHROOMS:
2 ½

WIDTH:
59' - 0"

DEPTH:
61' - 0"

FOUNDATION:
Crawlspace, Slab, Unfinished Basement

Order online at eplans.com

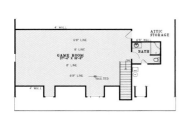

PLAN:
HPK3300137

SQUARE FOOTAGE:
1,921

BONUS SPACE:
812 sq. ft.

BEDROOMS:
3

BATHROOMS:
2

WIDTH:
84' - 0"

DEPTH:
55' - 6"

FOUNDATION:
Crawlspace, Slab, Unfinished Basement

PLAN:
HPK3300138

SQUARE FOOTAGE:
1,723

BONUS SPACE:
557 sq. ft.

BEDROOMS:
3

BATHROOMS:
2

WIDTH:
52' - 6"

DEPTH:
55' - 6"

FOUNDATION:
Crawlspace, Slab

PLAN:

HPK3300139

SQUARE FOOTAGE:
1,962

BONUS SPACE:
264 sq. ft.

BEDROOMS:
3

BATHROOMS:
2

WIDTH:
66' - 0"

DEPTH:
49' - 4"

FOUNDATION:
Unfinished Basement, Block

Order online at eplans.com

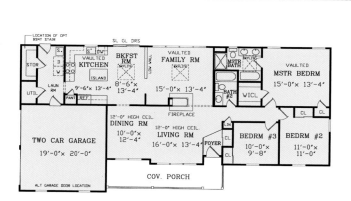

Optional Layout

PLAN:

HPK3300004

SQUARE FOOTAGE:
1,667

BEDROOMS:
3

BATHROOMS:
2

WIDTH:
70' - 0"

DEPTH:
34' - 4"

FOUNDATION:
Crawlspace, Slab, Unfinished Basement

Order online at eplans.com

PLAN:
HPK3300140

SQUARE FOOTAGE:
1,615

BEDROOMS:
3

BATHROOMS:
2

WIDTH:
72' - 4"

DEPTH:
32' - 4"

FOUNDATION:
Crawlspace, Slab, Unfinished Basement

Order online at eplans.com

A front porch and attractive gabled rooflines are both current and historic, fitting today's return to nostalgic styling. The living and dining rooms are wide open, enhancing the visual impression of lots of space. A dramatic cathedral ceiling highlights both rooms. Another highlight is a multisided fireplace that the living room shares with the rear-facing family room. The family room also features a cathedral ceiling, skylight, and rear window wall with a sliding glass door. There is also space for built-ins adjacent to the fireplace. A spacious U-shaped eat-in kitchen works around a center island. The adjacent breakfast area includes a double window to the rear yard. The kitchen also contains a cathedral ceiling and skylight. The master suite includes a walk-in closet, a spacious private bath with a double vanity, and a sloped ceiling with a skylight.

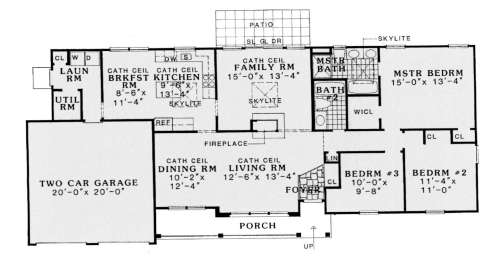

ORDER BLUEPRINTS 24 HOURS, 7 DAYS A WEEK, AT 1-800-521-6797 OR EPLANS.COM

ROOM TO STRETCH

Homes in the mid range of 2,000 to 2,800 square feet are ideal for a growing family or one with frequent guests. While smaller homes take advantage of rooms that perform double duty, the plans in this section come equipped with both formal and casual spaces. A living room greets visitors with seating for formal conversations, leaving the family or great room for laid-back activities. A dining room may house special occasions, whereas a smaller home may have a breakfast nook for all meals. Additional bedrooms and baths make friends and relatives feel more at home in these slightly larger plans.

For homeowners, the increase in square footage is most noticeable in the master bath. Here, a tub and a separate shower accommodate a couple's needs, along with a compartmented or hidden toilet. One or more walk-in closets will surely please, as will the extra space in the bedroom, possibly with room for a sitting area.

Outside, longer front porches may wrap around the home, making room for swings and chairs. Rear decks and patios may be larger, too, with designated activity zones. The facade may borrow exterior elements, such as gables and stone, from other styles, but the layout remains true to the traits that make ranch homes so appealing.

PLAN:
HPK3300141

SQUARE FOOTAGE:
2,201

BEDROOMS:
3

BATHROOMS:
3

WIDTH:
69' - 6"

DEPTH:
55' - 10"

Order online at eplans.com

Featuring a stunning exterior of stucco, stone, and cedar shakes, this home both blends with and takes advantage of the beauty of its natural surroundings. Designed for optimum openness, the common areas are defined by interior columns and ceiling heights. Windows extend dramatically across the back of the home for exceptional backyard views. The master suite features a tray ceiling, sitting alcove, and private bath with dual walk-in closets, garden tub, and separate shower. A bedroom/study, located adjacent to the master suite, has access to a hall bath, and a third bedroom, on the opposite side of the home, boasts its own private bath.

PLAN:
HPK3300142

SQUARE FOOTAGE:
2,663
BONUS SPACE:
653 sq. ft.
BEDROOMS:
4
BATHROOMS:
2 ½
WIDTH:
72'- 7"
DEPTH:
71'- 5"

Order online at eplans.com

This home's personality is reflected in charming arch-top windows, set off with keystones and decorative shutters. A columned foyer receives natural light from a clerestory window and opens to the great room, which boasts a cathedral ceiling and sliding glass doors to the sunroom. An extended-hearth fireplace adds warmth to the living area. Open planning allows the nearby gourmet kitchen to share the glow of the hearth. The breakfast room really lets the sunshine in with a triple window to the rear property. The master suite offers private access to the rear deck with a spa and features a cozy fireplace, a relaxing bath, and a generous walk-in closet. Three family bedrooms—or make one a study—share a full bath and a powder room on the other side of the plan.

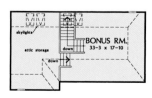

Rear Exterior

PLAN:
HPK3300143

SQUARE FOOTAGE:
2,017
BONUS SPACE:
360 sq. ft.
BEDROOMS:
3
BATHROOMS:
2
WIDTH:
57' - 0"
DEPTH:
70' - 0"

Order online at eplans.com

PLAN:
HPK3300144

SQUARE FOOTAGE:
2,358
BONUS SPACE:
324 sq. ft.
BEDROOMS:
4
BATHROOMS:
2
WIDTH:
65' - 8"
DEPTH:
68' - 10"

Order online at eplans.com

Rear Exterior

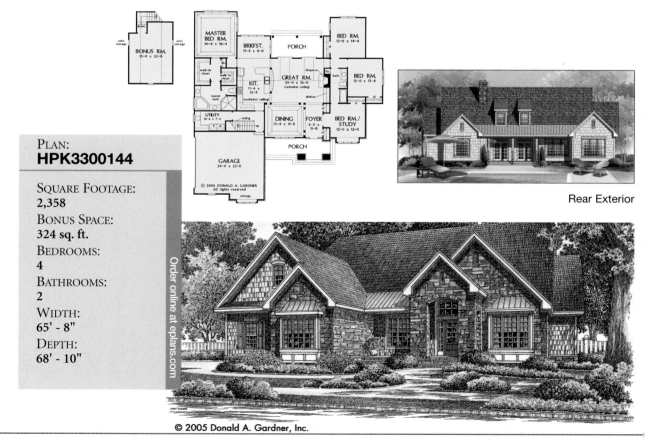

PLAN:
HPK3300145

SQUARE FOOTAGE:
2,369

BEDROOMS:
3

BATHROOMS:
2 ½

WIDTH:
56' - 0"

DEPTH:
70' - 4"

Rear Exterior

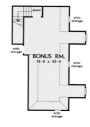

Rear Exterior

PLAN:
HPK3300146

SQUARE FOOTAGE:
2,645

BONUS SPACE:
543 sq. ft.

BEDROOMS:
3

BATHROOMS:
2 ½

WIDTH:
67' - 4"

DEPTH:
65' - 0"

PLAN:

HPK3300147

SQUARE FOOTAGE:
2,426
BEDROOMS:
4
BATHROOMS:
3
WIDTH:
73' - 2"
DEPTH:
58' - 0"

Order online at eplans.com

Gable-topped stone walls join low-maintenance siding and charming twin dormers for exceptional curb appeal. Palladian windows and columns add architectural interest, while front and rear porches take living to the great outdoors. Positioning gives rooms definition, while the floorplan remains open. Decorative ceiling treatments and interior columns accentuate the gathering rooms, and built-in cabinetry flanks the fireplace. Common rooms divide the master suite from the secondary bedroom wing, promoting privacy and tranquility for each bedroom. The master suite includes dual walk-in closets and a well-appointed bath. Versatility is provided by a flexible study/bedroom and bonus room above the garage.

© 2005 Donald A. Gardner, Inc.

An Arts and Crafts facade boasts elegant curb appeal as double dormers echo the dual-arched portico. Twin sets of tapered columns provide architectural detail in this lavish exterior. Vaulted ceilings in the great room offer generous height throughout the open living spaces. Ceiling treatments enhance the dining room and foyer, creating vertical volume. The master bedroom is flanked by a large rear porch that creates additional space for entertaining guests or enjoying Mother Nature. A vaulted ceiling, dual sinks, and walk-in closets give the master suite additional flair. Secondary bedrooms run parallel to one another and share a common bathroom.

Rear Exterior

PLAN:

HPK3300148

SQUARE FOOTAGE:
2,193

BEDROOMS:
3

BATHROOMS:
2

WIDTH:
56' - 4"

DEPTH:
73' - 0"

Order online at eplans.com

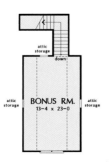

© 1995 Donald A. Gardner Architects, Inc.

Rear Exterior

PLAN:
HPK3300149

SQUARE FOOTAGE:
2,192
BONUS SPACE:
390 sq. ft.
BEDROOMS:
4
BATHROOMS:
2 ½
WIDTH:
74' - 10"
DEPTH:
55' - 8"

Order online at eplans.com

Volumes of windows and 9-foot ceilings add elegance to this comfortable open plan. Hosts whose guests always end up in the kitchen will enjoy entertaining here, with only columns separating it from the great room. Children's bedrooms share a full bath that's complete with a linen closet. The master suite, located in a quiet wing, is highlighted by a tray ceiling and includes a skylit bath with a garden tub, private toilet, double-bowl vanity, and spacious walk-in closet.

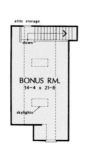

© 1998 Donald A. Gardner, Inc.

A trio of dormers and a front porch adorn the facade of this sprawling four-bedroom country home. Illuminated by the center dormer, the vaulted foyer gives way to the dining room with a tray ceiling and to the spacious great room with a cathedral ceiling, a fireplace, and built-in shelves. A split-bedroom layout provides privacy for homeowners in a generous master suite with a tray ceiling and private bath. Three additional bedrooms reside on the opposite side of the home.

PLAN:

HPK3300150

SQUARE FOOTAGE:
2,487

BEDROOMS:
4

BATHROOMS:
3

WIDTH:
86' - 2"

DEPTH:
51' - 8"

Order online at eplans.com

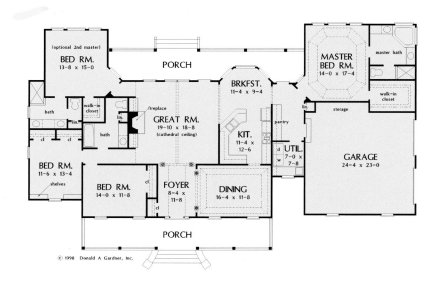

© 1998 Donald A Gardner, Inc.

PLAN:
HPK3300151

SQUARE FOOTAGE:
2,207
BONUS SPACE:
435 sq. ft.
BEDROOMS:
4
BATHROOMS:
2 ½
WIDTH:
76' - 1"
DEPTH:
50' - 0"

Order online at eplans.com

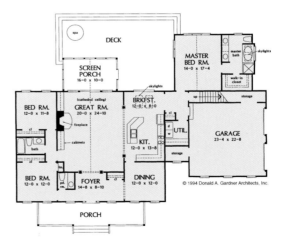

Rear Exterior

PLAN:
HPK3300152

SQUARE FOOTAGE:
2,136
BONUS SPACE:
405 sq. ft.
BEDROOMS:
3
BATHROOMS:
2 ½
WIDTH:
76' - 4"
DEPTH:
64' - 4"

Order online at eplans.com

© 1990 Donald A. Gardner, Architects, Inc

This enchanting design incorporates the best in floor planning all on one amenity-filled level. Large, arched windows and corner quoins lend a distinctly European flavor to the feeling of this brick-exterior home. A front porch framed by columns welcomes you inside to an inviting foyer. The central great room is the hub of the plan, from which all other rooms radiate. It is highlighted with a fireplace and cathedral ceiling. Nearby is a skylit sunroom with sliding glass doors to the rear deck and a built-in wet bar. The galley-style kitchen adjoins an attached breakfast room. The master suite is split from the family bedrooms and accesses the rear deck. The pampering master bath offers a whirlpool tub, separate shower, and twin-sink vanity. Family bedrooms on the opposite side of the house share a full hall bath. Extra storage space can be found in the two-car garage.

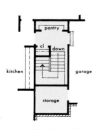

Rear Exterior

PLAN:
HPK3300153

SQUARE FOOTAGE:
2,099

BEDROOMS:
3

BATHROOMS:
2

WIDTH:
72' - 6"

DEPTH:
53' - 10"

Order online at eplans.com

© 1990 Donald A. Gardner Architects, Inc.

Optional Layout

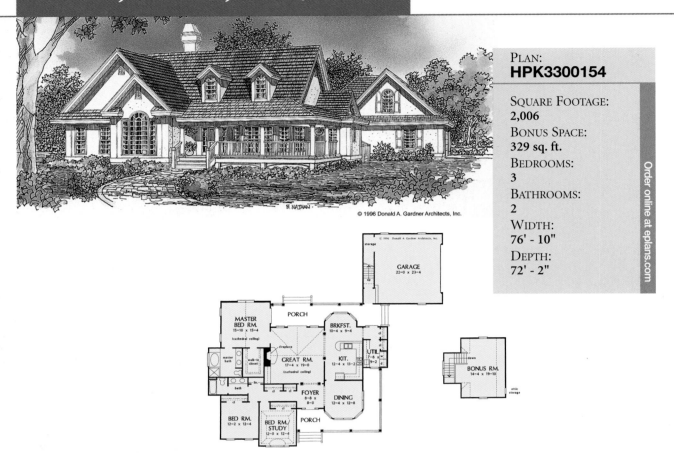

© 1996 Donald A. Gardner Architects, Inc.

PLAN:
HPK3300154

SQUARE FOOTAGE:
2,006
BONUS SPACE:
329 sq. ft.
BEDROOMS:
3
BATHROOMS:
2
WIDTH:
76' - 10"
DEPTH:
72' - 2"

Order online at eplans.com

PLAN:
HPK3300155

SQUARE FOOTAGE:
2,273
BONUS SPACE:
342 sq. ft.
BEDROOMS:
4
BATHROOMS:
2 ½
WIDTH:
74' - 8"
DEPTH:
75' - 10"

Order online at eplans.com

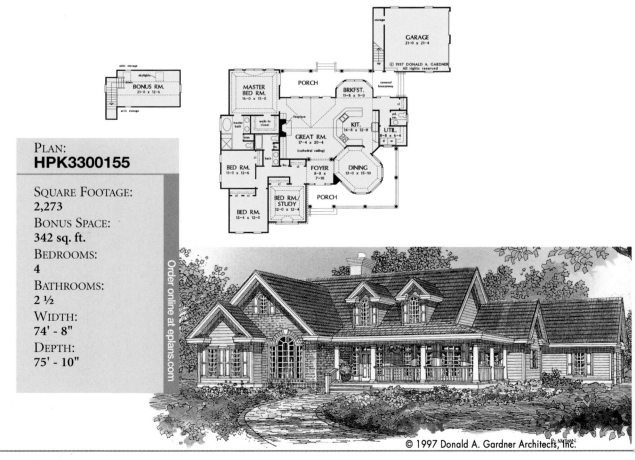

© 1997 Donald A. Gardner Architects, Inc.

PLAN:
HPK3300156

This traditional home features board-and-batten and cedar shingles in a well-proportioned, country-flavored exterior. The foyer opens to the dining room and leads to the great room, which offers French doors to the rear columned porch. An additional bedroom or study shares a full bath with Bedroom 2. The lavish master suite features a luxurious private bath and two walk-in closets. A fourth bedroom—or make it a home office—resides just off the kitchen.

SQUARE FOOTAGE:
2,090
BEDROOMS:
4
BATHROOMS:
3
WIDTH:
61' - 0"
DEPTH:
70' - 6"
FOUNDATION:
Finished Walkout Basement

Order online at eplans.com

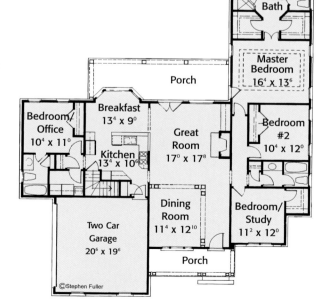

PLAN:
HPK3300157

SQUARE FOOTAGE:
2,090

BEDROOMS:
4

BATHROOMS:
3

WIDTH:
61' - 0"

DEPTH:
72' - 0"

FOUNDATION:
Finished Walkout Basement

Order online at eplans.com

This home's European styling will work well in a variety of environments. When it comes down to the details, this plan has it all. Begin with the front door, which opens into the dining and great rooms—the latter complete with a fireplace and doors that open to the back porch. The kitchen combines with the breakfast nook to create ample space for meals. This plan incorporates four bedrooms; you may want to use one as an office and another as a study. The master bedroom houses a fabulous bath with twin walk-in closets and a spa tub.

PLAN:
HPK3300158

SQUARE FOOTAGE:
2,295

BEDROOMS:
3

BATHROOMS:
2

WIDTH:
69' - 0"

DEPTH:
49' - 6"

FOUNDATION:
Unfinished Walkout Basement

Order online at eplans.com

The abundance of details in this plan makes it the finest in one-story living. The great room and formal dining room are loosely defined by a simple column at the entry foyer, allowing for an open, dramatic space. The kitchen with prep island shares the right side of the plan with a bayed breakfast area and a keeping room with a fireplace. Sleeping accommodations to the left of the plan include a master suite with a sitting area, two closets, and a separate tub and shower. Two family bedrooms share a full bath. Additional living and sleeping space can be developed in the walkout basement.

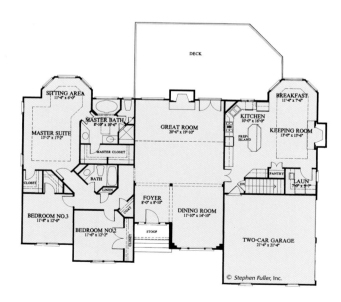

© Stephen Fuller, Inc.

© Stephen Fuller, Inc.

PLAN:
HPK3300159

SQUARE FOOTAGE:
2,377

BEDROOMS:
3

BATHROOMS:
2

WIDTH:
69' - 0"

DEPTH:
49' - 6"

FOUNDATION:
Finished Walkout Basement

Order online at eplans.com

One-story living takes a lovely traditional turn in this brick home. The entry foyer opens to the formal dining room and the great room through graceful columned archways. The open gourmet kitchen, bayed breakfast nook, and keeping room with a fireplace will be a magnet for family activity. Sleeping quarters offer two family bedrooms, a hall bath, and a rambling master suite with a bayed sitting area and a sensuous bath.

© Stephen Fuller, Inc.

This classic cottage boasts a stone-and-wood exterior with a welcoming arch-top entry that leads to a columned foyer. An extended-hearth fireplace is the focal point of the family room, and a nearby sunroom with covered porch access opens up the living area to the outdoors. The gourmet island kitchen opens through double doors from the living area; the breakfast area looks out to a porch. Sleeping quarters include a master wing with a spacious, angled bath and a sitting room or den that has its own full bath—perfect for a guest room. On the opposite side of the plan, two family bedrooms share a full bath.

PLAN:

HPK3300160

SQUARE FOOTAGE:
2,170
BEDROOMS:
4
BATHROOMS:
3
WIDTH:
62' - 0"
DEPTH:
61' - 6"
FOUNDATION:
Finished Walkout Basement

Order online at eplans.com

© Stephen Fuller, Inc.

PLAN:
HPK3300162

SQUARE FOOTAGE:
2,570

BEDROOMS:
3

BATHROOMS:
2 ½

WIDTH:
73' - 9"

DEPTH:
58' - 6"

FOUNDATION:
Unfinished Walkout Basement

Order online at eplans.com

Materials of stacked stone, stucco, and board and batten create a casual, rustic feel for this one-story home. The great room with fireplace and the master bedroom open to an intimate covered back porch. The kitchen opens to a keeping room and breakfast area with fireplace. All of the bedrooms are on the right side of the home; the two secondary bedrooms share a Jack-and-Jill bath while the master suite is situated in the rear for privacy. A large two-car garage completes the package.

©Stephen Fuller

This home warmly welcomes both family and visitors with its charming covered front porch and multipane windows. Inside, the formal dining room opens directly off the foyer and has access to the porch. At the back of the plan, a large country kitchen includes an island counter and opens to a bay-windowed breakfast area. Just off the kitchen is a comfortable great room enhanced by a fireplace, a beam ceiling, and access to a second covered porch. The luxurious master suite has many tempting amenities, such as a pampering bath, a huge walk-in closet, and access to the rear covered porch.

PLAN:
HPK3300163

SQUARE FOOTAGE:
2,796
BEDROOMS:
3
BATHROOMS:
2 ½
WIDTH:
70' - 9"
DEPTH:
66' - 6"
FOUNDATION:
Finished Walkout Basement

Order online at eplans.com

©Stephen Fuller

PLAN:

HPK3300164

SQUARE FOOTAGE:
2,236
BEDROOMS:
3
BATHROOMS:
2 ½
WIDTH:
63' - 0"
DEPTH:
67' - 0"
FOUNDATION:
Crawlspace, Unfinished Walkout Basement

Order online at eplans.com

PLAN:

HPK3300165

SQUARE FOOTAGE:
2,302
BONUS SPACE:
595 sq. ft.
BEDROOMS:
3
BATHROOMS:
2 ½
WIDTH:
69' - 0"
DEPTH:
53' - 0"
FOUNDATION:
Crawlspace, Unfinished Walkout Basement

Order online at eplans.com

ORDER BLUEPRINTS 24 HOURS, 7 DAYS A WEEK, AT 1-800-521-6797 OR EPLANS.COM

PLAN:

HPK3300166

This design is so comprehensive, you won't believe that there is bonus space included. A covered porch accesses a foyer with an adjoining open formal dining area leading to the stunning great room, past decorative columns. The master suite is partitioned to the right of the great room and features a stylish tray ceiling and luscious vaulted bath behind a French door. A separate bedroom is hidden away with its own bath. An ultra-functional kitchen lies to the left of the great room, with an open space adjoining the breakfast area to the latter. The nook opens to the patio via a French door and affords a panoramic outdoor view through a bay window. Around a built-in desk and walk-in pantry are the laundry room and two bedrooms that share a bath.

SQUARE FOOTAGE:
2,050

BONUS SPACE:
418 sq. ft.

BEDROOMS:
4

BATHROOMS:
3

WIDTH:
60' - 0"

DEPTH:
56' - 0"

FOUNDATION:
Crawlspace, Slab, Unfinished Walkout Basement

Order online at eplans.com

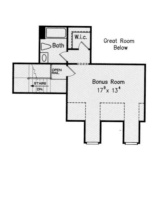

PLAN:

HPK3300167

SQUARE FOOTAGE:
2,568
BONUS SPACE:
303 sq. ft.
BEDROOMS:
4
BATHROOMS:
3
WIDTH:
66' - 0"
DEPTH:
61' - 0"
FOUNDATION:
Crawlspace, Slab, Unfinished Walkout Basement

Order online at eplans.com

A double-gabled portico over a covered front porch and shuttered, multipaned windows create a cheerful facade to this country cottage. Across the threshold is a foyer with an 11-foot-high ceiling, and a formal dining room that opens up to the right. A long hallway connects the wings of the plan. A vaulted family room with built-in cabinets, a fireplace, and a window wall faces the rear property. Open to the right of the family room is the kitchen and breakfast area, with a door to the outside. A convenient corner pantry, perfect for storage of food items and table linens, is stowed in the nook. The opulent, vaulted master wing resides on the left of the plan and includes an angled vanity counter and oversized tub as well as a generous walk-in closet. Bonus space upstairs is ideal for an additional bedroom suite.

PLAN:
HPK3300168

A stunning brick facade with classy Colonial touches conceals a smart interior. Maximum privacy is achieved by counterposing the luscious master suite and the twin bedrooms in opposite corners of the home. The intervening space is filled by a formal dining room and vaulted great room, both set off by stately columns as well as a spacious kitchen, breakfast nook, and cozy keeping room. Fireplaces bring warmth to the great room and the keeping room, while a series of windows along the back walls of these rooms fill them with natural light.

SQUARE FOOTAGE:
2,600
BONUS SPACE:
311 sq. ft.
BEDROOMS:
3
BATHROOMS:
2 ½
WIDTH:
57' - 0"
DEPTH:
70' - 0"
FOUNDATION:
Crawlspace, Slab, Unfinished Walkout Basement

Order online at eplans.com

PLAN:
HPK3300169

SQUARE FOOTAGE:
2,061
BEDROOMS:
3
BATHROOMS:
2 ½
WIDTH:
88' - 10"
DEPTH:
40' - 9"
FOUNDATION:
Crawlspace, Slab

Order online at eplans.com

This amazing home is detailed with sloped roofs, a stone facade, and muntin windows. Enjoy the stone fireplace whether relaxing in the great room or sipping a drink at the bar extended from the kitchen. Adjacent to the kitchen, a dining area includes sliding glass doors leading to a covered patio. A private patio area is available to the master bedroom, as well as a spacious private bath, which includes a double-bowl sink and a vast walk-in closet. Two family bedrooms each have double-door closets and share a full bath. A three-car garage resides to the far right of the plan, with an entryway opening to the utility room.

PLAN:
HPK3300170

SQUARE FOOTAGE:
2,439
BONUS SPACE:
390 sq. ft.
BEDROOMS:
3
BATHROOMS:
2 ½
WIDTH:
77' - 0"
DEPTH:
59' - 1"
FOUNDATION:
Crawlspace, Slab

Order online at eplans.com

This charmer is constructed with a shingle-and-stone facade. Fronted with rustic columns and a Tudor-style chimney, the exterior evokes images of a country farmhouse. The dormer windows allow for a brightened entry way on sunny days. On your left lies the great room with a vaulted ceiling. The kitchen is located to the left, joining forces with the breakfast area (the kitchen's best secret is a corner pantry). From here, there is also access to the covered patio. A formal dining room—also convertible to a study—opens off the gallery through an archway. Past two hall closets and a family bedroom on the right is the bonus staircase, for an upstairs attic or loft, and the master suite. A third bedroom and utility area also occupy this part of the floor.

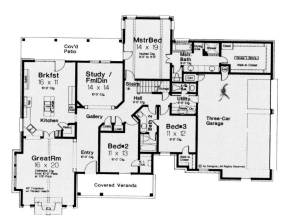

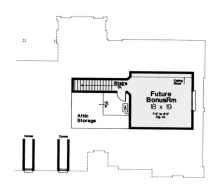

PLAN:
HPK3300171

SQUARE FOOTAGE:
2,696
BEDROOMS:
4
BATHROOMS:
3 ½
WIDTH:
80' - 0"
DEPTH:
64' - 1"
FOUNDATION:
Slab

Order online at eplans.com

A brick archway covers the front porch of this European-influenced home, creating a truly grand entrance. Situated beyond the entry, the living room takes center stage with a fireplace flanked by tall windows. To the right is a bayed eating area and an efficient kitchen. Steps away is the formal dining room. Skillful planning creates flexibility for the master suite. If you wish, use Bedroom 2 as a secondary bedroom or guest room, with the adjacent study accessible to everyone. Or, if you prefer, combine the master suite with the study and use it as a private retreat with Bedroom 2 as a nursery, creating a wing that provides total privacy. Completing this clever plan are two family bedrooms, a powder room, and a utility room.

ORDER BLUEPRINTS 24 HOURS, 7 DAYS A WEEK, AT 1-800-521-6797 OR EPLANS.COM

PLAN:
HPK3300172

SQUARE FOOTAGE:
2,590

BEDROOMS:
4

BATHROOMS:
3 ½

WIDTH:
73' - 6"

DEPTH:
64' - 10"

FOUNDATION:
Slab

Order online at eplans.com

With a solid exterior of rough cedar and stone, this new French Country design will stand the test of time. A wood-paneled study in the front features a large bay window. The heart of the house is found in a large open great room with a built-in entertainment center. The spacious master bedroom features a corner reading area and access to an adjacent covered patio. A three-car garage and three additional bedrooms complete this generous family home.

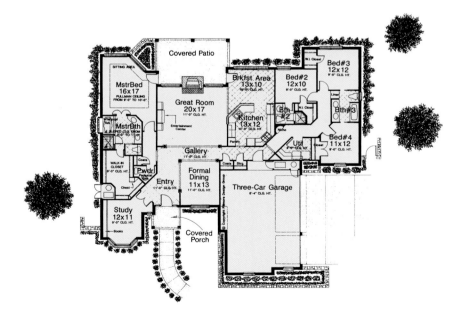

PLAN:
HPK3300173

SQUARE FOOTAGE:
2,063

BEDROOMS:
3

BATHROOMS:
2

WIDTH:
69' - 2"

DEPTH:
51' - 0"

FOUNDATION:
Unfinished Basement

Order online at eplans.com

Shadowed gables present a visual treat to passersby. Once inside, stand in the foyer and see the delightful open space created by the great room, dining room, and breakfast nook. Each room has its own personality, however, with unique ceiling treatments. An optional bedroom/library presents homeowners with numerous possibilities. Bedrooms are clustered on the right side of the plan and include a master suite with a private bath and two family bedrooms—or one bedroom and a library—that share a full bath.

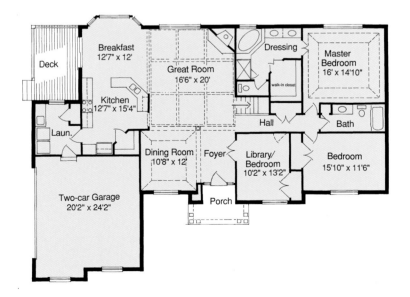

ORDER BLUEPRINTS 24 HOURS, 7 DAYS A WEEK, AT 1-800-521-6797 OR EPLANS.COM

PLAN:
HPK3300174

SQUARE FOOTAGE:
2,110

BEDROOMS:
3

BATHROOMS:
2

WIDTH:
92' - 6"

DEPTH:
56' - 8"

FOUNDATION:
Unfinished Walkout Basement

Order online at eplans.com

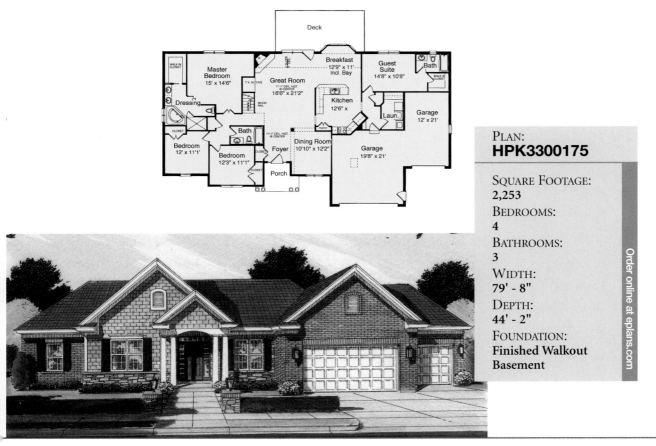

PLAN:
HPK3300175

SQUARE FOOTAGE:
2,253

BEDROOMS:
4

BATHROOMS:
3

WIDTH:
79' - 8"

DEPTH:
44' - 2"

FOUNDATION:
Finished Walkout Basement

Order online at eplans.com

PLAN:

HPK3300176

SQUARE FOOTAGE:
2,517

BEDROOMS:
3

BATHROOMS:
2 ½

WIDTH:
77' - 0"

DEPTH:
59' - 0"

Order online at eplans.com

This European stucco home is a well-designed one-story villa. Turrets top identical bayed rooms that are enclosed behind double doors just off the entry. The formal dining room and study are situated in the window-filled turrets. The family room is a spacious entertaining area with a fireplace and built-ins. An efficient kitchen is uniquely designed with its island and angular shape. The split-bedroom floor plan places the master suite away from the two family bedrooms.

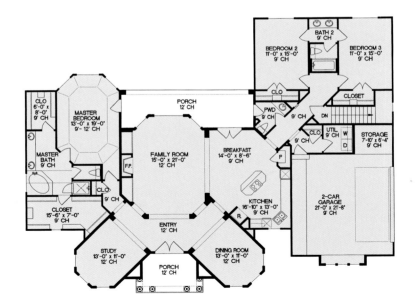

PLAN:

HPK3300177

SQUARE FOOTAGE:
2,242

BEDROOMS:
2

BATHROOMS:
2 ½

WIDTH:
64' - 0"

DEPTH:
64' - 0"

Order online at eplans.com

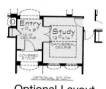

Optional Layout

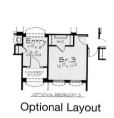

Optional Layout

Optional Layout

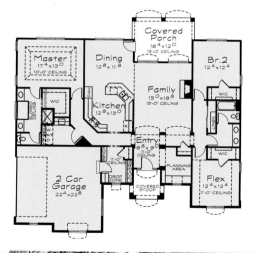

Optional Layout

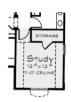

Optional Layout

PLAN:

HPK3300178

SQUARE FOOTAGE:
2,038

BEDROOMS:
3

BATHROOMS:
2

WIDTH:
59' - 0"

DEPTH:
58' - 0"

Order online at eplans.com

PLAN:
HPK3300179

SQUARE FOOTAGE:
2,311

BEDROOMS:
3

BATHROOMS:
2 ½

WIDTH:
64' - 0"

DEPTH:
57' - 2"

Order online at eplans.com

Interesting details on the front porch add to the appeal of this ranch home. The great room is highlighted by a pass-through wet bar/buffet and sits just across the hall from the formal dining room. A well-planned kitchen features a walk-in pantry and L-shaped island snack bar. The bedrooms are found in a cluster to the right of the home: a master suite, and two family bedrooms sharing a full bath. The master suite has a shower with glass-block detailing, a whirlpool tub, and dual vanities. A three-car garage attaches to the main house via an entrance near the utility room.

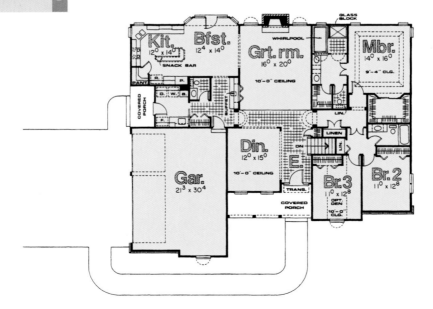

PLAN:

HPK3300180

G ently tapered columns set off an elegant arched entry framed by multipane windows. Inside, an open great room features a wet bar, fireplace, tall transom windows, and access to a covered porch with skylights. The gourmet kitchen boasts a food-preparation island and a snack bar and overlooks the gathering room. Double doors open to the master suite, where French doors lead to a private bath with an angled whirlpool tub and a sizable walk-in closet. One of two nearby family bedrooms could serve as a den, with optional French doors opening from a hall central to the sleeping wing.

SQUARE FOOTAGE:
2,456

BEDROOMS:
3

BATHROOMS:
2 ½

WIDTH:
66' - 0"

DEPTH:
68' - 0"

Order online at eplans.com

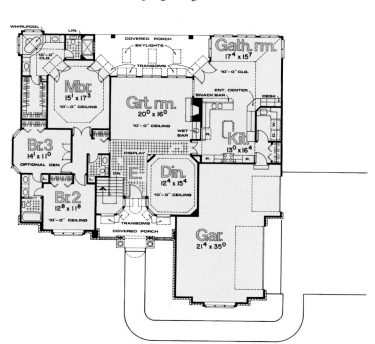

PLAN:

HPK3300181

SQUARE FOOTAGE:
2,538

BEDROOMS:
3

BATHROOMS:
2 ½

WIDTH:
68' - 8"

DEPTH:
64' - 8"

Order online at eplans.com

The grand front porch gives this home unique style and majestic curb appeal. Inside, the entry centers on the stately dining room with its bowed window. Both the living room and the second bedroom—which can be converted into a den—have 10-foot ceilings. The island kitchen features abundant storage space, a lazy Susan, and a snack bar. A sun-filled breakfast area opens to the large family room with its cathedral ceiling and central fireplace. The private bedroom wing offers two secondary bedrooms and a luxurious master suite featuring a spacious walk-in closet with built-in dressers, and private access to the backyard. The master bath includes a vaulted ceiling, a corner whirlpool tub, and His and Hers vanities.

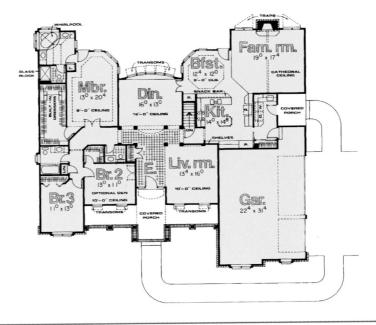

PLAN:
HPK3300182

SQUARE FOOTAGE:
2,172
BEDROOMS:
3
BATHROOMS:
3
WIDTH:
76' - 0"
DEPTH:
46' - 0"

Order online at eplans.com

This one-story home with grand rooflines contains a convenient floor plan. The great room with a fireplace complements a front-facing living room. The formal dining room with a tray ceiling sits just across the hall from the living room and is also easily accessible to the kitchen. An island, pantry, breakfast room, and patio are highlights in the kitchen. A bedroom at this end of the house works fine as an office or guest bedroom. Two additional bedrooms are to the right of the plan: a master suite with a grand bath and an additional family bedroom.

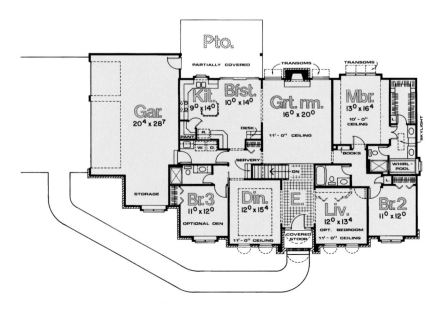

Photography Courtesy of Mark Englund. This home, as shown in the photography, may differ

PLAN:
HPK3300183

SQUARE FOOTAGE:
2,791

BEDROOMS:
4

BATHROOMS:
2

WIDTH:
84' - 0"

DEPTH:
54' - 0"

FOUNDATION:
Crawlspace, Slab

Order online at eplans.com

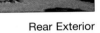

Rear Exterior

This stately country home is a quaint mix of Colonial style and romantic French flavor. Inside, formal living and dining rooms flank the entry foyer. Two sets of double doors open from the family room onto the rear patio. A romantic courtyard is placed to the far right of the plan, just beyond the family bedrooms. A three-car garage with an extra storage room offers plenty of space. The family game room is reserved for recreational fun.

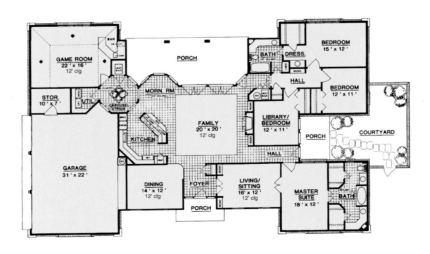

© 1996 William E Poole Designs, Inc.

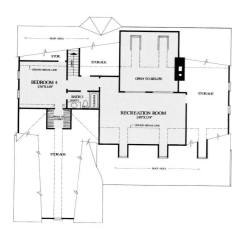

Country flavor is well established on this fine three-bedroom home. The covered front porch welcomes friends and family alike to the foyer, where the formal dining room opens to the left. The vaulted ceiling in the great room enhances the wall of windows with backyard views. An efficient kitchen blends well with the bayed breakfast area. The secluded master suite offers a walk-in closet and a lavish bath; on the other side of the home, two family bedrooms share a full bath. Upstairs, an optional fourth bedroom is available for guests or in-laws and provides access to a large recreation room.

PLAN:
HPK3300184

SQUARE FOOTAGE:
2,151
BONUS SPACE:
814 sq. ft.
BEDROOMS:
3
BATHROOMS:
2
WIDTH:
61' - 0"
DEPTH:
55' - 8"
FOUNDATION:
Crawlspace, Unfinished Basement

Order online at eplans.com

PLAN:

HPK3300185

SQUARE FOOTAGE:
2,549

BEDROOMS:
4

BATHROOMS:
2 ½

WIDTH:
88' - 8"

DEPTH:
53' - 6"

FOUNDATION:
Unfinished Basement

Order online at eplans.com

Covered porches to the front and rear will be the envy of the neighborhood when this house is built. The interior plan meets family needs perfectly in well-zoned areas. The sleeping wing has four bedrooms and two baths. The living zone has formal and informal gathering space. A work zone with a U-shaped kitchen shares space with the naturally lit breakfast nook. The laundry and powder room are located in the far right corner of the plan. The two-car garage has a huge storage area.

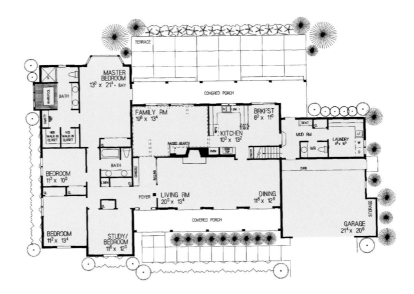

PLAN:
HPK3300186

SQUARE FOOTAGE:
2,261

BEDROOMS:
4

BATHROOMS:
2 ½

WIDTH:
85' - 8"

DEPTH:
46' - 0"

FOUNDATION:
Unfinished Basement

Order online at eplans.com

A privacy wall around the courtyard with a pool and trellised planter area is a gracious way by which to enter this one-story design. The Spanish flavor is accented by the grillwork and tiled roof. The front living room has sliding glass doors that open to the entrance court. The adjacent dining room features a bay window. Enjoy informal activities in the rear family room with a beamed ceiling, a raised-hearth fireplace, sliding glass doors to the terrace, and a snack bar. The sleeping wing can remain quiet away from the plan's activity centers. Notice the three-car garage with extra storage space.

PLAN:

HPK3300187

SQUARE FOOTAGE:
2,539

BEDROOMS:
3

BATHROOMS:
2 ½

WIDTH:
75' - 2"

DEPTH:
68' - 8"

FOUNDATION:
Slab

Order online at eplans.com

Enjoy this beautiful Western vacation home! Exposed rafter tails, arched porch detailing, massive paneled front doors, and stucco exterior walls enhance the Western character of this U-shaped ranch house. Double doors open to a spacious, slope-ceilinged art gallery. The quiet sleeping zone is comprised of an entire wing. The extra room at the front of this wing may be used for a den or an office. The dining room and kitchen are located at the opposite end of the plan. Indoor-outdoor living relationships are outstanding. The large, open courtyard is akin to the fabled Greek atrium. It is accessible from each of the zones and functions with a covered arbor, which looks out over the rear landscape. The master suite has a generous sitting area, a walk-in closet, twin lavatories, a whirlpool tub, and a stall shower.

PLAN:
HPK3300188

SQUARE FOOTAGE:
2,424

BEDROOMS:
3

BATHROOMS:
2 ½

WIDTH:
68' - 0"

DEPTH:
64' - 0"

FOUNDATION:
Unfinished Basement

Order online at eplans.com

This unique one-story plan seems tailor-made for a small family or for empty-nesters. Formal areas are situated well for entertaining—living room to the right and formal dining room to the left. A large family room to the rear accesses a rear wood deck and is warmed in the cold months by a welcome hearth. The U-shaped kitchen features an attached morning room for casual meals near the laundry and a washroom. The master suite sits to the right of the plan and has a walk-in closet and a fine bath. A nearby den opens to a private porch. Two family bedrooms on the other side of the home share a full bath.

PLAN:
HPK3300189

SQUARE FOOTAGE:
2,034
BEDROOMS:
3
BATHROOMS:
2
WIDTH:
75' - 0"
DEPTH:
47' - 5"
FOUNDATION:
Unfinished Basement

Order online at eplans.com

Horizontal siding, multipane windows, and a spindled railing lend a prairies-and-plains flavor to this traditional home. A roomy foyer with a sloped ceiling and built-in shelves leads through a tiled vestibule with built-in shelves to the spacious gathering room, complete with a warming fireplace. An angled kitchen with a snack bar easily serves the formal dining room, which leads outdoors to the rear entertainment terrace. The luxurious master suite has its own door to the terrace, as well as a fabulous private bath with a windowed whirlpool tub. Two additional bedrooms share a full bath and a hall that offers more wardrobe space. One of the family bedrooms could serve as a study or home office.

A covered porch, shutters and a centered dormer with an arched window dress up this country home with blue-ribbon style. To the left of the foyer, the family room features a built-in entertainment center and a bay window that provides a window seat overlooking the front yard. Nearby, the kitchen—angled for interest—contains a pantry and a snack bar that opens to the adjacent living room and dining room. From here, access is provided to the rear covered porch, supplying a spacious area for outdoor dining. Split planning places the restful master suite to the rear for privacy. Amenities include a large walk-in closet and a soothing master bath with a whirlpool tub, separate shower, and double-bowl vanity.

PLAN:

HPK3300190

SQUARE FOOTAGE:
2,415

BEDROOMS:
4

BATHROOMS:
2 ½

WIDTH:
74' - 0"

DEPTH:
54' - 0"

FOUNDATION:
Unfinished Basement

Order online at eplans.com

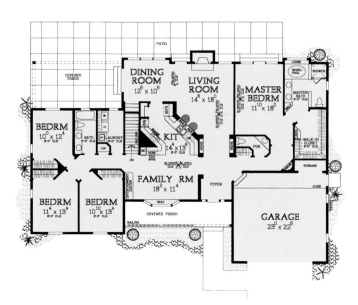

PLAN:
HPK3300191

SQUARE FOOTAGE:
2,090
BEDROOMS:
3
BATHROOMS:
2 ½
WIDTH:
84' - 6"
DEPTH:
64' - 0"
FOUNDATION:
Crawlspace

Order online at eplans.com

This classic farmhouse has a wraparound porch that's perfect for enjoying the outdoors. To the rear of the plan, a sun terrace with a spa opens from the master suite and the morning room. A great room offers a sloped ceiling and a corner fireplace with a raised hearth. A low wall and graceful archways set off by decorative columns define the formal dining room. The tiled kitchen has a center island counter with a snack bar and adjoins a laundry area. Two family bedrooms reside to the side of the plan, and each has private access to the covered porch. A secluded master suite nestles in its own wing and features a sitting area with access to the rear terrace and spa.

ORDER BLUEPRINTS 24 HOURS, 7 DAYS A WEEK, AT 1-800-521-6797 OR EPLANS.COM

PLAN:
HPK3300192

SQUARE FOOTAGE:
2,076

BEDROOMS:
3

BATHROOMS:
2

WIDTH:
64' - 8"

DEPTH:
54' - 7"

FOUNDATION:
Unfinished Basement

Order online at eplans.com

Multipane windows, mock shutters, and a covered front porch exhibit the charm of this home's facade. Inside, the foyer is flanked by a spacious, efficient kitchen to the right and a large, convenient laundry room to the left. The living room features a warming fireplace. To the right of the living room is the formal dining room; both rooms share a snack bar and direct access to the kitchen. Sleeping quarters are split, with two family bedrooms and a full bath on the right side of the plan and the deluxe master suite on the left. The private master bath offers such luxuries as a walk-in closet, a twin-sink vanity, and a separate tub and shower.

PLAN:
HPK3300193

SQUARE FOOTAGE:
2,086

BEDROOMS:
3

BATHROOMS:
2

WIDTH:
82' - 0"

DEPTH:
58' - 4"

FOUNDATION:
Slab

Order online at eplans.com

A majestic facade makes this home pleasing to view. The design provides dual-use space in the wonderful sunken sitting room and media area. The kitchen has a breakfast bay and overlooks the snack bar to the sunken family area. A few steps from the kitchen is the formal dining room, which functions well with the upper patio. Two family bedrooms share a full bath. The private master suite includes a sitting area and French doors that open to a private covered patio.

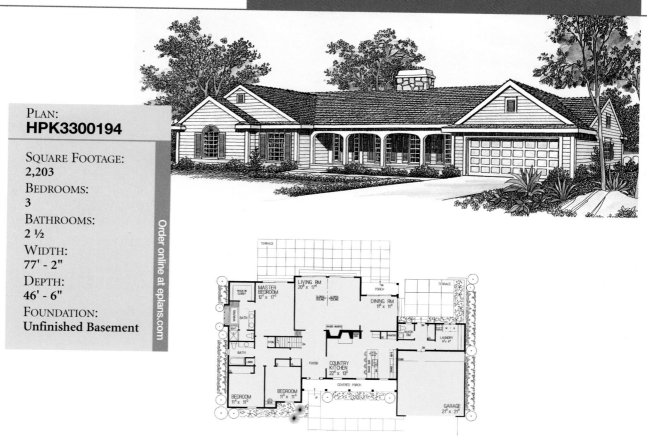

PLAN:
HPK3300194

SQUARE FOOTAGE:
2,203

BEDROOMS:
3

BATHROOMS:
2 ½

WIDTH:
77' - 2"

DEPTH:
46' - 6"

FOUNDATION:
Unfinished Basement

Order online at eplans.com

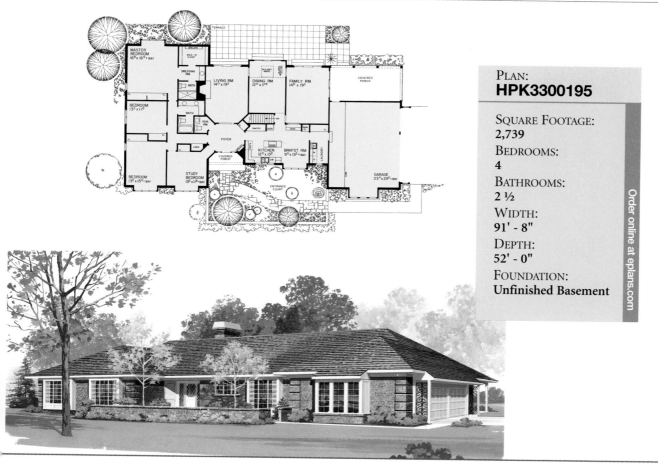

PLAN:
HPK3300195

SQUARE FOOTAGE:
2,739

BEDROOMS:
4

BATHROOMS:
2 ½

WIDTH:
91' - 8"

DEPTH:
52' - 0"

FOUNDATION:
Unfinished Basement

Order online at eplans.com

PLAN:
HPK3300196

SQUARE FOOTAGE:
2,547
BEDROOMS:
4
BATHROOMS:
2 ½
WIDTH:
74' - 8"
DEPTH:
56' - 8"
FOUNDATION:
Crawlspace, Unfinished Basement

Order online at eplans.com

A brick exterior with traditional arch details and elegant rooflines defines this stately ranch home. Formal dining and living rooms open through arches from the front entry foyer. Chefs can utilize their talents in the spacious kitchen with its center cooktop island, abundant counter space, and light-filled breakfast nook. The family room is separated from the kitchen by a snack counter and features a corner fireplace and double doors to the rear patio. The private master suite, separated from family bedrooms, offers a walk-in closet and a luxurious bath with a whirlpool spa, oversized shower, twin vanities, and compartmented toilet. Three additional bedrooms allow design flexibility—use one as a guest room, den, or home office.

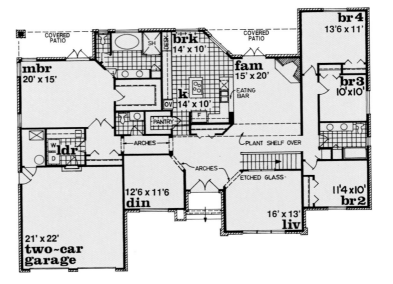

PLAN:

HPK3300197

This contemporary Craftsman-style bungalow fits right in beside an ocean, lake, or suburban neighborhood. Plenty of natural light beams into the vaulted foyer through sidelights and a wide transom. Double doors on the left access a vaulted room that could be a den or home office. The foyer opens to the spacious living room, where windows fill most of the rear wall. Opposite the corner gas fireplace, two openings lead to the kitchen and dinette. A long, raised eating bar is great for snacking, chatting, and homework supervision. In the kitchen, there's plenty of counter and cupboard space, built-in appliances, and a walk-in pantry. In the far corner of the home, the master suite features a luxury bath and patio access. Two secondary bedrooms and a bath open from a small hallway off the foyer.

SQUARE FOOTAGE:
2,103
BONUS SPACE:
414 sq. ft.
BEDROOMS:
3
BATHROOMS:
2
WIDTH:
66' - 0"
DEPTH:
64' - 0"
FOUNDATION:
Crawlspace

Order online at eplans.com

PLAN:
HPK3300198

SQUARE FOOTAGE:
2,270
BEDROOMS:
3
BATHROOMS:
2
WIDTH:
70' - 0"
DEPTH:
69' - 0"
FOUNDATION:
Crawlspace

Order online at eplans.com

Covered Patio

Patio

Dining

Coffered Owners' Suite 14'6" x 17'2"

Vaulted Great Room 36' x 17'4"

Living

Kitchen

Utility

Bedroom 11'8" x 11'4"

Vaulted Media/Study 12'6" x 12'8"

Vaulted Entry

Garage 33' x 23'

Porch

Vaulted Bedroom 14' x 12'

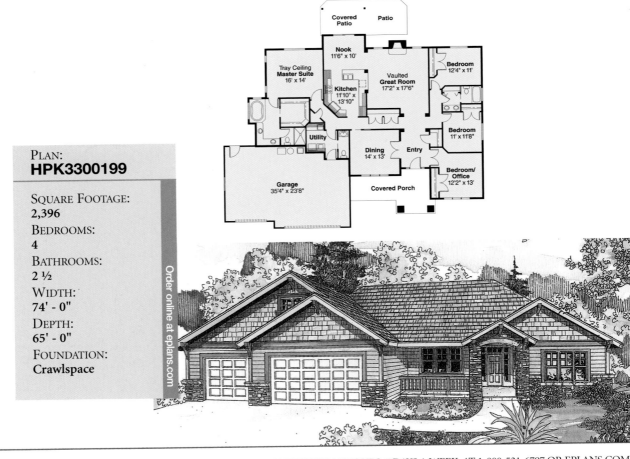

Covered Patio   **Patio**

Nook 11'6" x 10'

Tray Ceiling Master Suite 16' x 14'

Kitchen 11'10" x 13'10"

Vaulted Great Room 17'2" x 17'6"

Bedroom 12'4" x 11'

Utility

Bedroom 11' x 11'8"

Dining 14' x 13'

Entry

Garage 35'4" x 23'8"

Covered Porch

Bedroom/ Office 12'2" x 13'

PLAN:
HPK3300199

SQUARE FOOTAGE:
2,396
BEDROOMS:
4
BATHROOMS:
2 ½
WIDTH:
74' - 0"
DEPTH:
65' - 0"
FOUNDATION:
Crawlspace

Order online at eplans.com

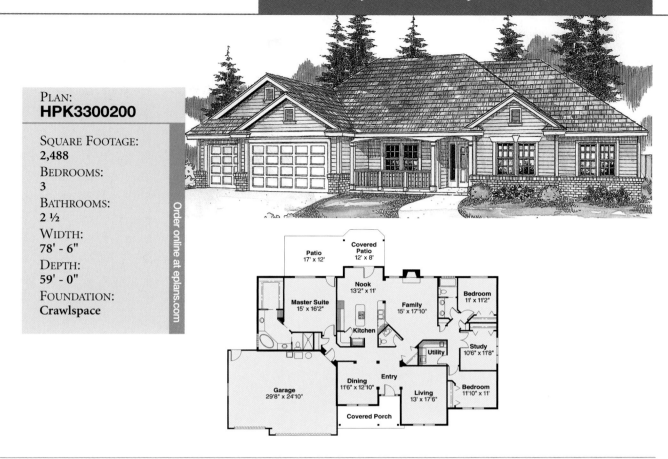

PLAN:
HPK3300200

SQUARE FOOTAGE:
2,488

BEDROOMS:
3

BATHROOMS:
2 ½

WIDTH:
78' - 6"

DEPTH:
59' - 0"

FOUNDATION:
Crawlspace

Order online at eplans.com

PLAN:
HPK3300201

SQUARE FOOTAGE:
2,653

BEDROOMS:
3

BATHROOMS:
2 ½

WIDTH:
84' - 0"

DEPTH:
66' - 0"

FOUNDATION:
Crawlspace

Order online at eplans.com

PLAN:

HPK3300202

SQUARE FOOTAGE:
2,392

BEDROOMS:
4

BATHROOMS:
2 ½

WIDTH:
67' - 2"

DEPTH:
71' - 8"

FOUNDATION:
Crawlspace, Slab, Unfinished Basement

Order online at eplans.com

PLAN:

HPK3300203

SQUARE FOOTAGE:
2,075

BEDROOMS:
4

BATHROOMS:
3

WIDTH:
66' - 0"

DEPTH:
52' - 0"

FOUNDATION:
Crawlspace, Slab

Order online at eplans.com

ORDER BLUEPRINTS 24 HOURS, 7 DAYS A WEEK, AT 1-800-521-6797 OR EPLANS.COM

PLAN:
HPK3300204

SQUARE FOOTAGE:
2,032

BEDROOMS:
3

BATHROOMS:
2

WIDTH:
58' - 0"

DEPTH:
58' - 2"

FOUNDATION:
Crawlspace, Slab

Order online at eplans.com

PLAN:
HPK3300205

SQUARE FOOTAGE:
2,264

BEDROOMS:
3

BATHROOMS:
2

WIDTH:
60' - 8"

DEPTH:
62' - 0"

FOUNDATION:
Slab

Order online at eplans.com

PLAN:
HPK3300206

SQUARE FOOTAGE:
2,249

BONUS SPACE:
553 sq. ft.

BEDROOMS:
3

BATHROOMS:
2 ½

WIDTH:
72' - 6"

DEPTH:
55' - 4"

FOUNDATION:
Slab

Order online at eplans.com

A large covered porch beckons those warm evenings sitting in the rocker enjoying the surrounding neighborhood ambiance. Upon entry, notice the vista view through the home to the covered patio and the rear yard beyond. To the right is the formal dining room with trayed ceiling and large buffet niche. To the left is the study, easily converted to a living room. The family room has a fireplace and space for a built-in media center. The secondary bedrooms share a semi-private bath. The master suite enters off the vestibule next to the nook, which also provides access to the bonus room over the garage and the laundry area. Note the built-in niche. The master suite is large and has access to the covered patio as well as the well-appointed master bath with a large walk-in closet. The master bath includes a corner tub, walk-in shower, private toilet chamber, and dual vanities with a center make-up area.

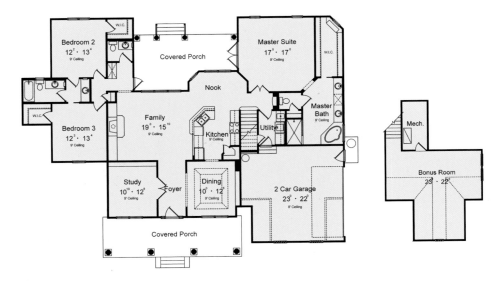

PLAN:
HPK3300207

SQUARE FOOTAGE:
2,265

BEDROOMS:
3

BATHROOMS:
2 ½

WIDTH:
90' - 0"

DEPTH:
45' - 8"

FOUNDATION:
Unfinished Basement

Order online at eplans.com

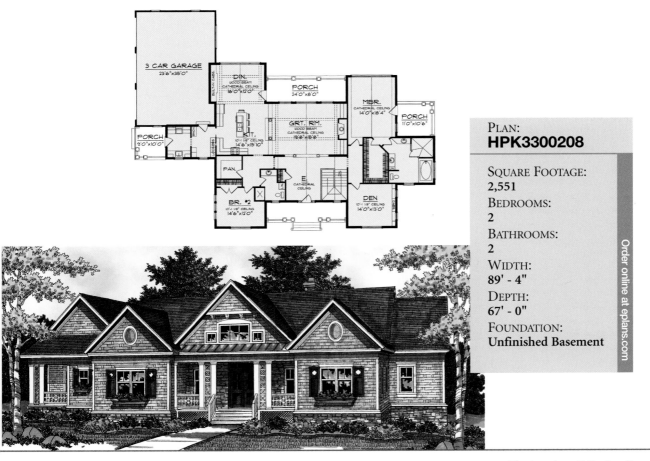

PLAN:
HPK3300208

SQUARE FOOTAGE:
2,551

BEDROOMS:
2

BATHROOMS:
2

WIDTH:
89' - 4"

DEPTH:
67' - 0"

FOUNDATION:
Unfinished Basement

Order online at eplans.com

© Larry E. Belk Designs

PLAN:
HPK3300209

SQUARE FOOTAGE:
2,733
BEDROOMS:
4
BATHROOMS:
2 ½
WIDTH:
88' - 0"
DEPTH:
54' - 2"
FOUNDATION:
Crawlspace, Slab

PLAN:
HPK3300210

SQUARE FOOTAGE:
2,506
BEDROOMS:
3
BATHROOMS:
2 ½
WIDTH:
89' - 6"
DEPTH:
54' - 2"
FOUNDATION:
Crawlspace, Slab

© Larry E. Belk Designs

PLAN:
HPK3300211

SQUARE FOOTAGE:
2,517
BEDROOMS:
4
BATHROOMS:
2 ½
WIDTH:
69' - 0"
DEPTH:
63' - 6"
FOUNDATION:
Crawlspace, Slab

Order online at eplans.com

A graceful stucco arch supported by columns gives this home instant curb appeal. Stucco quoins are used to further accent its traditional brick finish. Inside, the angled foyer steps down into the living room and draws the eye to a duplicate of the exterior arch with columns. Step down again to enter the formal dining room. The kitchen features a coffered ceiling and is conveniently grouped with a sunny bayed breakfast room and a family room, the perfect place for informal gatherings. Upon entering the master suite, the master bath becomes the focal point. Columns flank the entry to this luxurious bath with a whirlpool tub as its centerpiece, His and Hers walk-in closets, a separate shower, and double-bowl vanities.

PLAN:

HPK3300212

SQUARE FOOTAGE:
2,018
BEDROOMS:
3
BATHROOMS:
2
WIDTH:
74' - 11"
DEPTH:
49' - 2"
FOUNDATION:
Crawlspace, Slab,
Unfinished Basement

Porch
17-10x10-0

Master
Bedroom
13-0x17-1

M.Bath

Bath

Greatroom
21-0x16-3

Kitchen
13-0x14-0

Breakfast
13-3x8-11

Desk

Laun.
6-0x7-1

Stor.
8-1x7-1

Garage
20-11x21-5

Bedroom
13-0x11-3

Bedroom
13-1x14-1

Foyer

Dining
13-0x10-11

Porch
22-11x5-10

PLAN:

HPK3300213

SQUARE FOOTAGE:
2,465
BEDROOMS:
4
BATHROOMS:
2 ½
WIDTH:
65' - 1"
DEPTH:
73' - 7"
FOUNDATION:
Crawlspace, Slab,
Unfinished Basement

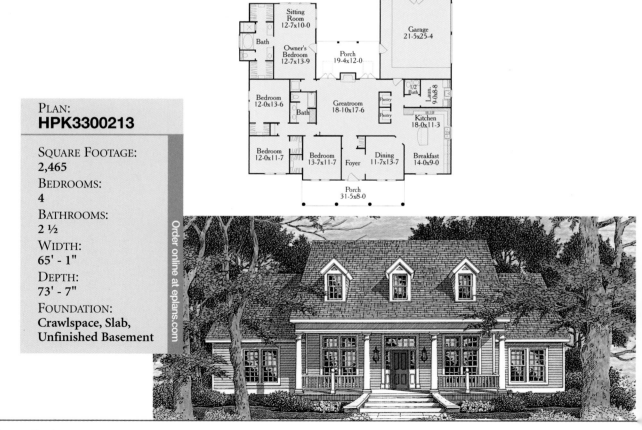

Storage
21-5x7-6

Sitting
Room
12-7x10-0

Bath

Owner's
Bedroom
12-7x13-9

Porch
19-4x12-0

Garage
21-5x25-4

Bedroom
12-0x13-6

Bath

Greatroom
18-10x17-6

Pantry

Pantry

1/2
Bath

Laun.
9-0x8-8

Kitchen
18-0x11-3

Bedroom
12-0x11-7

Bedroom
13-7x11-7

Foyer

Dining
11-7x13-7

Breakfast
14-0x9-0

Porch
31-5x8-0

This home's facade employs an elegant balance of country comfort and traditional grace. Inside, the foyer opens to the formal dining room that features a coffered ceiling. Straight ahead, the great room offers a warm fireplace and open flow to the breakfast and kitchen areas. Two secondary bedrooms and a full bath can be found just off the kitchen. A bonus room, near the master suite, can be used as a nursery or den. The private master bath includes dual vanities, two walk-in closets, and a compartmented toilet. Upstairs, unfinished space is ready for expansion.

PLAN:

HPK3300214

SQUARE FOOTAGE:
2,127

BONUS SPACE:
1,095 sq. ft.

BEDROOMS:
3

BATHROOMS:
2 ½

WIDTH:
69' - 0"

DEPTH:
67' - 4"

FOUNDATION:
Crawlspace, Slab, Unfinished Basement

Order online at eplans.com

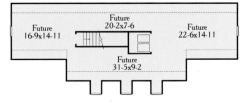

© Larry E. Belk Designs

PLAN:

HPK3300215

SQUARE FOOTAGE:
2,684

BONUS SPACE:
265 sq. ft.

BEDROOMS:
3

BATHROOMS:
2

WIDTH:
71' - 10"

DEPTH:
71' - 2"

FOUNDATION:
Crawlspace, Slab, Unfinished Basement

Order online at eplans.com

This well-proportioned Southern Colonial home begins with a welcoming porch and expands into the perfect family plan. On either side of the foyer are the study and the dining room; the study is functional and smart with built-in bookshelves, and the dining room is adorned with elegant columns. Arches and columns mark the entry to the family room, where a cozy fireplace framed by windows invites relaxation. The kitchen is equipped with a central cooktop island, a built-in planning desk, and a serving bar. Tucked away to encourage peace and quiet, the master suite delights in a lavish bath with a Roman tub. On the opposite side of the home, generous secondary bedrooms share a Jack-and-Jill bath.

ORDER BLUEPRINTS 24 HOURS, 7 DAYS A WEEK, AT 1-800-521-6797 OR EPLANS.COM

© Larry E. Belk Designs

A gabled stucco entry with oversized columns emphasizes the arched glass entry of this winsome one-story brick home. Arched windows on either side of the front door add symmetry and style to this pleasing exterior. An arched passage leads to the three family bedrooms and is flanked by twin bookcases and a plant ledge, providing focal interest to the living room. Bedroom 4 may also be used as a study and can be entered from double French doors off the living room. A large, efficient kitchen shares space with an octagonal breakfast area and a family room with a fireplace. Enter the master bedroom through angled double doors and view the cathedral ceiling. Attention centers immediately on the arched entry to the relaxing master bath and its central whirlpool tub.

PLAN:
HPK3300216

SQUARE FOOTAGE:
2,540
BEDROOMS:
4
BATHROOMS:
2 ½
WIDTH:
70' - 0"
DEPTH:
65' - 0"
FOUNDATION:
Crawlspace, Slab

Order online at eplans.com

PLAN:
HPK3300217

SQUARE FOOTAGE:
2,267

BEDROOMS:
4

BATHROOMS:
2 ½

WIDTH:
71' - 2"

DEPTH:
62' - 0"

FOUNDATION:
Crawlspace, Slab, Unfinished Basement

Order online at eplans.com

Six columns and a steeply pitched roof lend elegance to this four-bedroom home. To the right of the foyer, the dining area sits conveniently near the efficient island kitchen that offers plenty of work space. Natural light will flood the breakfast nook through a ribbon of windows facing the rear yard. Escape to the relaxing master bedroom, with its luxurious bath set between His and Hers walk-in closets. The great room is complete with a warming fireplace and built-ins. Three family bedrooms include private walk-in closets and share a fully appointed bath.

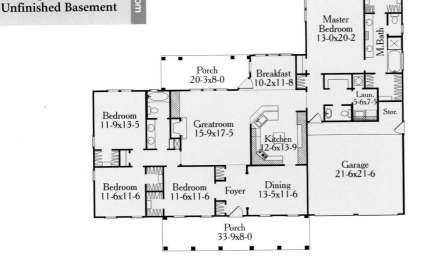

Basement Stair Location

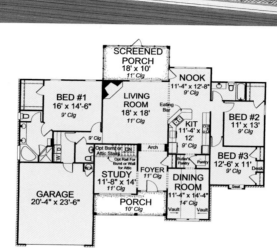

PLAN:

HPK3300218

SQUARE FOOTAGE:
2,140

BEDROOMS:
3

BATHROOMS:
2 ½

WIDTH:
68' - 0"

DEPTH:
58' - 0"

Order online at eplans.com

SCREENED PORCH 18' x 10' 11' Clg

NOOK 11'-4" x 12'-8" 9' Clg

BED #1 16' x 14'-6" 9' Clg

LIVING ROOM 18' x 18' 11' Clg

Eating Bar

KIT 11'-4' x 12' 9' Clg

BED #2 11' x 13' 9' Clg

Opt Bsmt or Attic Stairs

Opt Rail For Bsmt or Wall for Attic

Arch

Butler Pantry

Pantry

BED #3 12'-6" x 11' 9' Clg

Desk

STUDY 11'-8" x 14' 11' Clg

FOYER 11' Clg

DINING ROOM 11'-4" x 14'-4" 14' Clg

Seat

GARAGE 20'-4" x 23'-6"

PORCH 10' Clg

Vault

Vault

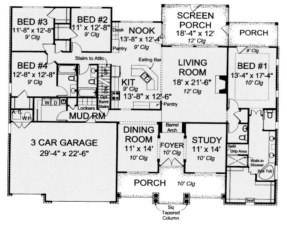

BED #3 11'-8" x 12'-8" 9' Clg

BED #2 11' x 12'-8" 9' Clg

Desk

NOOK 13'-8" x 12'4 9' Clg

SCREEN PORCH 18'-4" x 12' 12' Clg

PORCH

Pantry

Stairs to Attic

BED #4 12'-8" x 12'-8" 9' Clg

LIVING ROOM 18' x 21'-6" 12' Clg

9' Clg

BED #1 13'-4" x 17'-4" 10' Clg

Eating Bar

KIT 13'-8" x 12'-6"

Bsmt Stairs

Opt

Pantry

Lockers

W D

W.H.

MUD RM

Barrel Arch

DINING ROOM 11' x 14' 10' Clg

FOYER 10' Clg

STUDY 11' x 14' 10' Clg

Seat Drip Area

Walk-in Shower

Spa Tub

3 CAR GARAGE 29'-4" x 22'-6"

PORCH 10' Clg

Sq Tapered Column

Seat

PLAN:

HPK3300219

SQUARE FOOTAGE:
2,695

BEDROOMS:
4

BATHROOMS:
3 ½

WIDTH:
74' - 0"

DEPTH:
57' - 0"

Order online at eplans.com

PLAN:
HPK3300220

SQUARE FOOTAGE:
2,340
BONUS SPACE:
296 sq. ft.
BEDROOMS:
3
BATHROOMS:
2 ½
WIDTH:
59' - 0"
DEPTH:
64' - 0"

Order online at eplans.com

A pleasing cottage exterior reveals an interior open layout of family-oriented rooms. The living room is central to the design, with a corner fireplace and access to a rear screened porch. The breakfast nook and kitchen are located at the front of the plan, encouraging guests to sit and chat amid the home's bustling activities. The master suite is thoughtfully placed on the left side of the plan, away from the remaining family bedrooms on the right. The suite includes a large master bath, a wide walk-in closet, and its own access to the porch. The two secondary bedrooms, behind the dining room, share a full hall bath with a double vanity. Nearby stairs lead up to the optional game room.

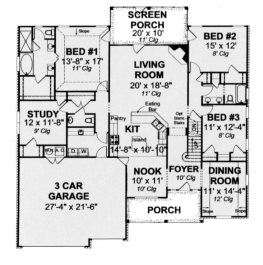

ORDER BLUEPRINTS 24 HOURS, 7 DAYS A WEEK, AT 1-800-521-6797 OR EPLANS.COM

Here's a great country house that's packed with modern amenities. From the foyer to the rear-loading garage, this plan provides high style and a deep level of comfort. Formal rooms offer tall views and share an open space defined by decorative columns. The casual living area includes a spacious family room with a fireplace. The gourmet kitchen has a peninsula counter with a snack bar. A vaulted eating nook leads out to the rear covered porch—a perfect opportunity to enjoy the sunrise while eating breakfast. The master suite boasts a dual vanity and a box-bay window.

PLAN:
HPK3300221

SQUARE FOOTAGE:
2,227
BEDROOMS:
3
BATHROOMS:
2
WIDTH:
50' - 0"
DEPTH:
71' - 0"
FOUNDATION:
Crawlspace

Order online at eplans.com

Photo by: Bob Greenspan. This home as shown in the photography, may differ from the actual

PLAN:

HPK3300222

SQUARE FOOTAGE:
2,775

BEDROOMS:
3

BATHROOMS:
2 ½

WIDTH:
74' - 0"

DEPTH:
59' - 0"

FOUNDATION:
Crawlspace

Order online at eplans.com

A quaint dining gazebo adds a delightful touch to the facade of this lovely home. It complements the formal living room, with a fireplace, found just to the right of the entry foyer (be sure to notice the elegant guest bath to the left). Family living takes place at the rear of the plan in a large family room with a through-fireplace to the study. A breakfast nook enhances the well-appointed kitchen. The master suite has a vaulted ceiling and boasts a huge walk-in closet and a pampering bath. Two family bedrooms share a full bath.

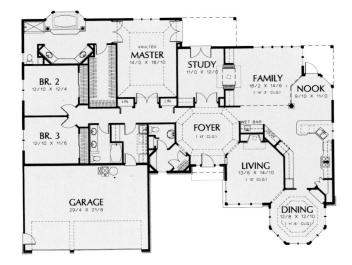

PLAN:

HPK3300223

W onderful, thoughtful touches abound throughout this home....What will your favorite be? The vaulted great room, surrounded by columns and warmed by a cozy hearth? Perhaps the open island-cooktop kitchen and light-filled nook that reveals a stunning side porch, perfect for summer dining? Telecommuters, students, and Web surfers are sure to love the office, tucked away for quietness yet convenient to the two rear bedrooms and a powder room. The master suite is a dream come true, with a vaulted bedroom, indulgent spa bath, and an ultraconvenient walk-in closet that accesses the laundry room directly. A three-car garage with extra storage space completes this fantastic plan.

SQUARE FOOTAGE:
2,650
BEDROOMS:
3
BATHROOMS:
2 ½
WIDTH:
94' - 0"
DEPTH:
53' - 0"
FOUNDATION:
Crawlspace

Order online at eplans.com

PLAN:
HPK3300224

SQUARE FOOTAGE:
2,001

BEDROOMS:
3

BATHROOMS:
2

WIDTH:
60' - 0"

DEPTH:
50' - 0"

FOUNDATION:
Crawlspace

Order online at eplans.com

With the security and comfort found in traditional American homes, this lovely design combines fresh country style with old-fashioned values. From the arched entry, the foyer leads inside to a sprawling great room with vaulted ceilings, a fireplace, and an optional media center. The open kitchen easily serves the dining area, complete with a hutch (or choose built-ins). Looking out over the rear property, the master suite includes a vaulted ceiling, pampering spa bath, and abundant closet space. Two bedrooms at the front of the home share an angled bath; a nearby den may also be used as a fourth bedroom. A two- or three-car garage accommodates a shop area for the do-it-yourselfer.

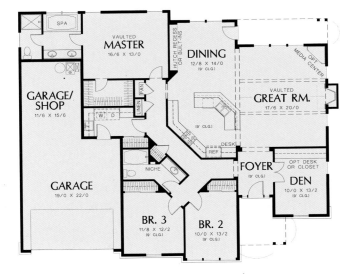

PLAN:
HPK3300225

SQUARE FOOTAGE:
2,260

BEDROOMS:
3

BATHROOMS:
3

WIDTH:
62' - 0"

DEPTH:
69' - 2"

FOUNDATION:
Unfinished Basement

Order online at eplans.com

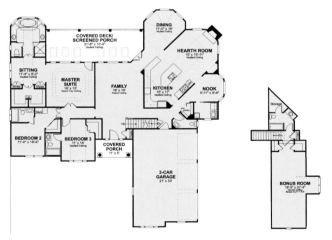

PLAN:
HPK3300226

SQUARE FOOTAGE:
2,461

BEDROOMS:
3

BATHROOMS:
3 ½

WIDTH:
71' - 4"

DEPTH:
74' - 8"

FOUNDATION:
Unfinished Basement

Order online at eplans.com

PLAN:
HPK3300227

SQUARE FOOTAGE:
2,483

BEDROOMS:
3

BATHROOMS:
2

WIDTH:
69' - 0"

DEPTH:
53' - 8"

FOUNDATION:
Unfinished Basement

Order online at eplans.com

This elegant traditional home is distinguished by its brick exterior and arched entryway with keystone accent. The entryway opens on the right to a formal dining room with an attractive tray ceiling. On the left, a private study—or make it a fourth bedroom—boasts a vaulted ceiling and a picture window with sunburst transom. Family living space includes a vaulted great room with a corner fireplace and a gourmet kitchen with an adjacent breakfast room. Special features in the kitchen include a breakfast bar, center island, menu desk, and pantry. The fabulous master suite features a bay window, large bath, walk-in closet, and vaulted ceiling. Two family bedrooms sharing a full hall bath complete the plan. An unfinished basement provides room for future expansion.

WIDE, WELCOME SPACES

© The Sater Collection, Inc.

Designers of the plans in this section began with simple ranch designs and expanded them into single-story luxuries, meant to pamper and please. From the exquisite exterior accents to the opulent interior amenities, from Craftsman inspirations to Mediterranean dreams, a home over 2,800 square feet is not your average ranch.

Some of these homes appear to be larger versions of previous ranch plans, while others take the style to the next level by adding elements from other genres. Stucco exteriors resemble Mediterranean villas; Ionic columns bring Colonial styles to mind; brick and gables form single-level manors; and exposed beams derive from turn-of-the-century Craftsman homes. There is no limit to the potential of these designs.

Inside, vaulted ceilings increase height, even in a one-story home. Multiple entertainment rooms, such as media rooms, treat family and friends. The master suite is the icing on the cake, with His and Hers closets, garden tubs, standing showers, and dual vanities. A stone hearth or French door to the patio may even grace the bedroom.

Outside there are summer kitchens and fireplaces for alfresco dining and cool evenings. Italian-inspired designs may take a lanai-side pool into account, as well may homes suited to the English countryside. The traditional ranch layout is no longer restrained to a specific look, but can live within a multitude of exterior styles.

PLAN:

HPK3300228

SQUARE FOOTAGE:
3,163

BEDROOMS:
3

BATHROOMS:
2

WIDTH:
77' - 8"

DEPTH:
72' - 4"

FOUNDATION:
Slab

Order online at eplans.com

This home lights up inside with a unique array of skylights. Enter through the foyer, graced by a skylit tower, to the living room and the warmth of a fireplace. Flanking the foyer is a skylight gallery; to the left is a master suite with a private den, two spacious walk-in closets, His and Hers vanities, a skylit shower, and a spa tub. On the right, the dining room, two family bedrooms that share a bath, the skylit family room, gourmet kitchen, and breakfast nook complete this attractive plan. Two separate garages are set to the rear with entry through the laundry room.

ORDER BLUEPRINTS 24 HOURS, 7 DAYS A WEEK, AT 1-800-521-6797 OR EPLANS.COM

PLAN:
HPK3300229

SQUARE FOOTAGE:
3,163

BEDROOMS:
4

BATHROOMS:
3 ½

WIDTH:
75' - 2"

DEPTH:
68' - 8"

FOUNDATION:
Slab

Order online at eplans.com

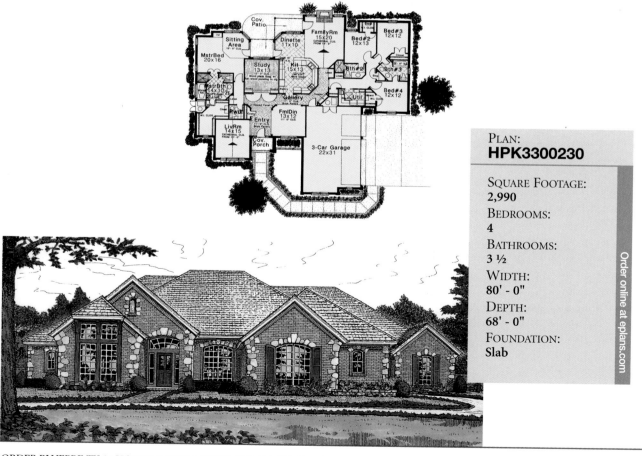

PLAN:
HPK3300230

SQUARE FOOTAGE:
2,990

BEDROOMS:
4

BATHROOMS:
3 ½

WIDTH:
80' - 0"

DEPTH:
68' - 0"

FOUNDATION:
Slab

Order online at eplans.com

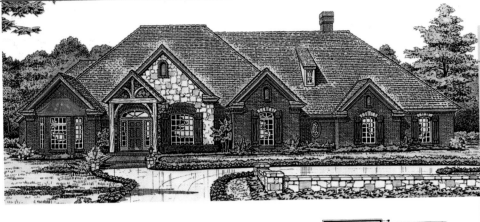

PLAN:
HPK3300231

SQUARE FOOTAGE:
3,352

BEDROOMS:
4

BATHROOMS:
3 ½

WIDTH:
91' - 0"

DEPTH:
71' - 9"

FOUNDATION:
Crawlspace, Slab

Order online at eplans.com

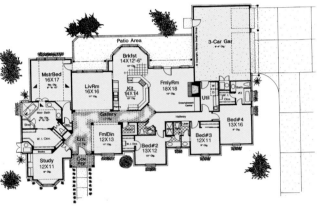

PLAN:
HPK3300232

SQUARE FOOTAGE:
3,270

BEDROOMS:
4

BATHROOMS:
3 ½

WIDTH:
101' - 0"

DEPTH:
48' - 1"

FOUNDATION:
Crawlspace, Slab

Order online at eplans.com

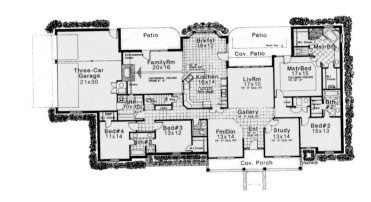

PLAN:

HPK3300233

SQUARE FOOTAGE:
3,394

BONUS SPACE:
816 sq. ft.

BEDROOMS:
4

BATHROOMS:
3 ½

WIDTH:
83' - 0"

DEPTH:
77' - 0"

FOUNDATION:
Crawlspace, Unfinished Walkout Basement

Order online at eplans.com

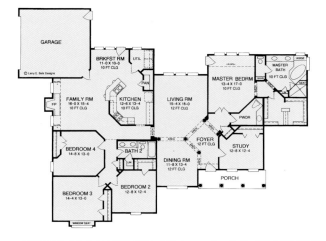

PLAN:

HPK3300234

SQUARE FOOTAGE:
2,846

BEDROOMS:
4

BATHROOMS:
2 ½

WIDTH:
84' - 6"

DEPTH:
64' - 2"

FOUNDATION:
Crawlspace, Slab

Order online at eplans.com

© Larry E. Belk Designs

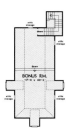

Rear Exterior

PLAN:
HPK3300235

SQUARE FOOTAGE:
3,068
BONUS SPACE:
746 sq. ft.
BEDROOMS:
3
BATHROOMS:
2 ½
WIDTH:
78' - 4"
DEPTH:
86' - 3"

Order online at eplans.com

Rear Exterior

PLAN:
HPK3300236

SQUARE FOOTAGE:
3,080
BONUS SPACE:
498 sq. ft.
BEDROOMS:
4
BATHROOMS:
4 ½
WIDTH:
75' - 7"
DEPTH:
72' - 3"

Order online at eplans.com

© 2005 Donald A. Gardner, Inc.

PLAN:
HPK3300237

SQUARE FOOTAGE:
2,820

BONUS SPACE:
473 sq. ft.

BEDROOMS:
4

BATHROOMS:
3

WIDTH:
78' - 1"

DEPTH:
65' - 5"

Order online at eplans.com

Rear Exterior

© 2005 DONALD A. GARDNER
All rights reserved

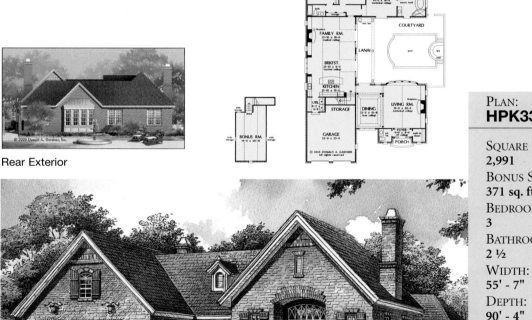

Rear Exterior

© 2005 Donald A. Gardner, Inc.

© 2005 DONALD A. GARDNER
All rights reserved

PLAN:
HPK3300238

SQUARE FOOTAGE:
2,991

BONUS SPACE:
371 sq. ft.

BEDROOMS:
3

BATHROOMS:
2 ½

WIDTH:
55' - 7"

DEPTH:
90' - 4"

Order online at eplans.com

© 2004 Donald A. Gardner, Inc.

Rear Exterior

PLAN:

HPK3300239

SQUARE FOOTAGE:
2,934

BEDROOMS:
4

BATHROOMS:
3

WIDTH:
85' - 4"

DEPTH:
57' - 8"

Order online at eplans.com

Starting with a massive front porch covered with a metal roof, a prominent gable with a Palladian window and decorative bracket, and two bay windows with French doors, this home evokes a rugged sophistication. Inside, positioning and architectural features give room definition while keeping an open floorplan. Tray ceilings top the versatile study/bedroom, master bedroom, dining room, and breakfast nook, while an angled counter separates the kitchen from the great room and breakfast nook. A vaulted ceiling caps the great room, expanding visual space. The common rooms divide the master suite from the secondary bedrooms, promoting peace and quiet. Two large walk-in closets provide plenty of storage space, while the well-equipped master bath includes twin vanities, a private privy, garden tub, and spacious shower.

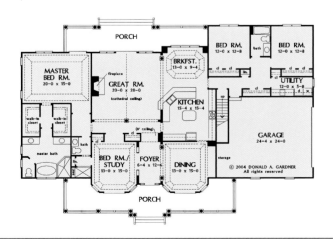

PLAN:

HPK3300240

This spacious one-story home easily accommodates a large family, providing all the luxuries and necessities for gracious living. For formal occasions, a grand dining room sits just off the entry foyer and features a vaulted ceiling. The great room offers a beautiful ceiling treatment and access to the rear deck. For more casual times, the kitchen, breakfast nook, and adjoining keeping room with a fireplace fit the bill. The master suite is spacious and filled with amenities that include a sitting room, walk-in closet, and access to the rear deck. Two family bedrooms share a full bath.

SQUARE FOOTAGE:
2,935
BEDROOMS:
3
BATHROOMS:
2 ½
WIDTH:
71' - 0"
DEPTH:
66' - 0"
FOUNDATION:
Finished Walkout Basement

Order online at eplans.com

© The Sater Collection, Inc.

PLAN:
HPK3300241

SQUARE FOOTAGE:
3,398
BEDROOMS:
3
BATHROOMS:
3 ½
WIDTH:
121' - 5"
DEPTH:
96' - 2"
FOUNDATION:
Slab

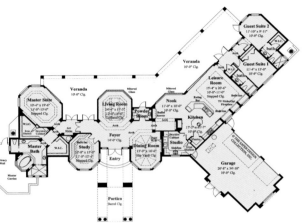

PLAN:
HPK3300242

SQUARE FOOTAGE:
2,962
BEDROOMS:
4
BATHROOMS:
3
WIDTH:
70' - 0"
DEPTH:
76' - 0"
FOUNDATION:
Slab

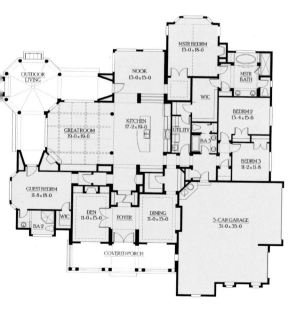

Rear Exterior

PLAN:
HPK3300243

SQUARE FOOTAGE:
3,500
BEDROOMS:
4
BATHROOMS:
3
WIDTH:
87' - 0"
DEPTH:
86' - 6"
FOUNDATION:
Crawlspace

Stunning exterior architecture complements the dramatic interiors of this elegant beauty. The gracious columned front porch leads to a carefully crafted floor plan with warm living spaces and spacious covered porches highlighted by columns and ceiling details. Intimate private suites are full of luxurious features and ample storage. Laundry access from the large master walk-in closet is a special convenience. The grand kitchen and adjacent great room make a bold statement upon entry. A fireplace in the outdoor living area is an added bonus.

House Plans— Super Sized

Hanley Wood has compiled the best-selling and most popular home plans into the most extensive home plan resources available. Now delivering more of everything you want—more plans, more styles and more choices—your dream home is right around the corner.

If you are looking to build a new home, look to Hanley Wood first. Pick up a copy today!

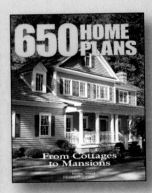

With more than 50 years of experience in the industry and millions of blueprints sold, Hanley Wood is a trusted source of high-quality, high-value pre-drawn home plans.

Using pre-drawn home plans is a **reliable, cost-effective way** to build your dream home, and our vast selection of plans is second-to-none. The nation's finest designers craft these plans that builders know they can trust. Meanwhile, our friendly, knowledgeable customer service representatives can help you every step of the way.

WHAT YOU'LL GET WITH YOUR ORDER

The contents of each designer's blueprint package is unique, but all contain detailed, high-quality working drawings. You can expect to find the following standard elements in most sets of plans:

I. FRONT PERSPECTIVE

This artist's sketch of the exterior of the house gives you an idea of how the house will look when built and landscaped.

2. FOUNDATION AND BASEMENT PLANS

This sheet shows the foundation layout including concrete walls, footings, pads, posts, beams, bearing walls, and foundation notes. If the home features a basement, the first-floor framing details may also be included on this plan. If your plan features slab construction rather than a basement, the plan shows footings and details for a monolithic slab. This page, or another in the set, may include a sample plot plan for locating your house on a building site. Additional sheets focus on foundation cross-sections and other details.

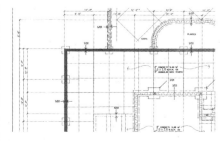

3. DETAILED FLOOR PLANS

These plans show the layout of each floor of the house. Rooms and interior spaces are carefully dimensioned, doors and windows located, and keys are given for cross-section details provided elsewhere in the plans.

4. HOUSE AND DETAIL CROSS-SECTIONS

Large-scale views show sections or cutaways of the foundation, interior walls, exterior walls, floors, stairways, and roof details. Additional cross-sections may show important changes in floor, ceiling, or roof heights, or the relationship of one level to another. These sections show exactly how the various parts of the house fit together and are extremely valuable during construction. Additional sheets may include enlarged wall, floor, and roof construction details.

5. FLOOR STRUCTURAL SUPPORTS

The floor framing plans provide detail for these crucial elements of your home. Each includes floor joist, ceiling joist, spacing, direction, span, and specifications. Beam and window headers, along with necessary details for framing connections, stairways, or dormers are also included.

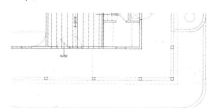

6. ELECTRICAL PLAN

The electrical plan offers suggested locations with notes for all lighting, outlets, switches, and circuits. A layout is provided for each level, as well as basements, garages, or other structures. This plan does not contain diagrams detailing how all wiring should be run, or how circuits should be engineered. These details should be designed by your electrician.

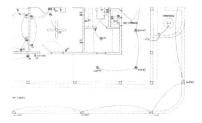

7. EXTERIOR ELEVATIONS

In addition to the front exterior, your blueprint set will include drawings of the rear and sides of your house as well. These drawings give notes on exterior materials and finishes. Particular attention is given to cornice detail, brick and stone accents, or other finish items that make your home unique.

ROOF FRAMING PLANS — PLEASE READ

Some plans contain roof framing plans; however because of the wide variation in local requirements, many plans do not. If you buy a plan without a roof framing plan, you will need an engineer familiar with local building codes to create a plan to build your roof. Even if your plan does contain a roof framing plan, we recommend that a local engineer review the plan to verify that it will meet local codes.

BEFORE YOU CALL

You are making a terrific decision to use a pre-drawn house plan—it is one you can make with confidence, knowing that your blueprints are crafted by national-award-winning certified residential designers and architects, and trusted by builders.

Once you've selected the plan you want—or even if you have questions along the way—our experienced customer service representatives are available 24 hours a day, seven days a week to help you navigate the home-building process. To help them provide you with even better service, please consider the following questions before you call:

■ Have you chosen or purchased your lot?

If so, please review the building setback requirements of your local building authority before you call. You don't need to have a lot before ordering plans, but if you own land already, please have the width and depth dimensions handy when you call.

■ Have you chosen a builder?

Involving your builder in the plan selection and evaluation process may be beneficial. Luckily, builders know they can have confidence with pre-drawn plans because they've been designed for livability, functionality, and typically are builder-proven at successful home sites across the country.

■ Do you need a construction loan?

Construction loans are unique because they involve determining the value of something that is not yet constructed. Several lenders offer convenient contstruction-to-permanent loans. It is important to choose a good lending partner—one who will help guide you through the application and appraisal process. Most will even help you evaluate your contractor to ensure reliability and credit worthiness. Our partnership with IndyMac Bank, a nationwide leader in construction loans, can help you save on your loan, if needed.

■ How many sets of plans do you need?

Building a home can typically require a number of sets of blueprints—one for yourself, two or three for the builder and subcontractors, two

for the local building department, and one or more for your lender. For this reason, we offer 5- and 8-set plan packages, but your best value is the Reproducible Plan Package. Reproducible plans are accompanied by a license to make modifications and typically up to 12 duplicates of the plan so you have enough copies of the plan for everyone involved in the financing and construction of your home.

■ Do you want to make any changes to the plan?

We understand that it is difficult to find blueprints for a home that will meet all of your needs. That is why Hanley Wood is glad to offer plan Customization Services. We will work with you to design the modifications you'd like to see and to adjust your blueprint plans accordingly—anything from changing the foundation; adding square footage, redesigning baths, kitchens, or bedrooms; or most other modifications. This simple, cost-effective service saves you from hiring an outside architect to make alterations. Modifications may only be made to Reproducible Plan Packages that include the license to modify.

■ Do you have to make any changes to meet local building codes?

While all of our plans are drawn to meet national building codes at the time they were created, many areas required that plans be stamped by a local engineer to certify that they meet local building codes. Building codes are updated frequently and can vary by state, county, city, or municipality. Contact your local building inspection department, office of planning and zoning, or department of permits to determine how your local codes will affect your construction project. The best way to assure that you can make changes to your plan, if necessary, is to purchase a Reproducible Plan Package.

■ Has everyone—from family members to contractors—been involved in selecting the plan?

Building a new home is an exciting process, and using pre-drawn plans is a great way to realize your dreams. Make sure that everyone involved has had an opportunity to review the plan you've selected. While Hanley Wood is the only plans provider with an exchange policy, it's best to be sure all parties agree on your selection before you buy.

CALL TOLL-FREE 1-800-521-6797

Source Key
HPK33

CUSTOMIZE YOUR PLAN — HANLEY WOOD CUSTOMIZATION SERVICES

Creating custom home plans has never been easier and more directly accessible. Using state-of-the-art technology and top-performing architectural expertise, Hanley Wood delivers on a long-standing customer commitment to provide world-class home-plans and customization services. Our valued customers—professional home builders and individual home owners—appreciate the convenience and accessibility of this interactive, consultative service.

With the Hanley Wood Customization Service you can:

■ Save valuable time by avoiding drawn-out and frequently repetitive face-to-face design meetings

■ Communicate design and home-plan changes faster and more efficiently
■ Speed-up project turn-around time
■ Build on a budget without sacrificing quality
■ Transform master home plans to suit your design needs and unique personal style

All of our design options and prices are impressively affordable. A detailed quote is available for a $50 consultation fee. Plan modification is an interactive service. Our skilled team of designers will guide you through the customization process from start to finish making recommendations, offering ideas, and determining the feasibility of your changes. This level of service is offered to ensure the final modified plan meets your expectations. If you use our service the $50 fee will be applied to the cost of the modifications.

You may purchase the customization consultation before or after purchasing a plan. In either case, it is necessary to purchase the Reproducible Plan Package and complete the accompanying license to modify the plan before we can begin customization.

Customization Consultation $50

TOOLS TO WORK WITH YOUR BUILDER

Two Reverse Options For Your Convenience — Mirror and Right-Reading Reverse (as available)

Mirror reverse plans simply flip the design 180 degrees—keep in mind, the text will also be flipped. For a minimal fee you can have one or all of your plans shipped mirror reverse, although we recommend having at least one regular set handy. Right-reading reverse plans show the design flipped 180 degrees but the text reads normally. When you choose this option, we ship each set of purchased blueprints in this format.

Mirror Reverse Fee (indicate the number of sets when ordering). . . . $55
Right Reading Reverse Fee (all sets are reversed). $175

A Shopping List Exclusively for Your Home — Materials List

A customized Materials List helps you plan and estimate the cost of your new home, outlining the quantity, type, and size of materials needed to build your house (with the exception of mechanical system items). Included are framing lumber, windows and doors, kitchen and bath cabinetry, rough and finished hardware, and much more.

Materials List . . . . $85 each
Additional Materials Lists (at original time of purchase only). . $20 each

Plan Your Home- Building Process — Specification Outline

Work with your builder on this step-by-step chronicle of 166 stages or items crucial to the building process. It provides a comprehensive review of the construction process and helps you choose materials.
Specification Outline . . . . $10 each

Learn the Basics of Building — Electrical, Plumbing, Mechanical, Construction Detail Sheets

If you want to know more about building techniques—and deal more confidently with your subcontractors—we offer four useful detail sheets. These sheets provide non-plan-specific general information, but are excellent tools that will add to your understanding of Plumbing Details, Electrical Details, Construction Details, and Mechanical Details.

Electrical Detail Sheet $14.95
Plumbing Detail Sheet $14.95
Mechanical Detail Sheet $14.95
Construction Detail Sheet $14.95
SUPER VALUE SETS:
Buy any 2: $26.95; Buy any 3: $34.95; Buy All 4: $39.95

Best Value

MAKE YOUR HOME TECH-READY — HOME AUTOMATION UPGRADE

Building a new home provides a unique opportunity to wire it with a plan for future needs. A Home Automation-Ready (HA-Ready) home contains the wiring substructure of tomorrow's connected home. It means that every room—from the front porch to the backyard, and from the attic to the basement—is wired for security, lighting, telecommunications, climate control, home computer networking, whole-house audio, home theater, shade control, video surveillance, entry access control, and yes, video gaming electronic solutions.

Along with the conveniences HA-Ready homes provide, they also have a higher resale value. The Consumer Electronics Association (CEA), in conjunction with the Custom Electronic Design and Installation Association (CEDIA), have developed a TechHome™ Rating system that quantifies the value of HA-Ready homes. The rating system is gaining widespread recognition in the real estate industry.

Developed by CEDIA-certified installers, our Home Automation Upgrade package includes everything you need to work with an installer during the construction of your home. It provides a short explanation of the various subsystems, a wiring floor plan for each level of your home, a detailed materials list with estimated costs, and a list of CEDIA-certified installers in your local area.

Home Automation Upgrade $250

GET YOUR HOME PLANS PAID FOR!

IndyMac Bank, in partnership with Hanley Wood, will reimburse you up to $750 toward the cost of your home plans simply by financing the construction of your new home with IndyMac Bank Home Construction Lending.

IndyMac's construction and permanent loan is a one-time close loan, meaning that one application—and one set of closing fees—provides all the financing you need.

Apply today at www.indymacbank.com, call toll free at 1-800-847-6138, or ask a Hanley Wood customer service representative for details.

DESIGN YOUR HOME — INTERIOR AND EXTERIOR FINISHING TOUCHES

Be Your Own Interior Designer! — Home Furniture Planner

Effectively plan the space in your home using our Hands-On Home Furniture Planner. It's fun and easy—no more moving heavy pieces of furniture to see how the room will go together. The kit includes reusable peel-and-stick furniture templates that fit on a 12"x18" laminated layout board—enough space to lay out every room in your house.

Home Furniture Planning Kit $15.95

Enjoy the Outdoors! — Deck Plans

Many of our homes have a corresponding deck plan, sold separately, which includes a Deck Plan Frontal Sheet, Deck Framing and Floor Plans, Deck Elevations, and a Deck Materials List. A Standard Deck Details Package, also available, provides all the how-to information necessary for building any deck. Get both the Deck Plan and the Standard Deck Details Package for one low price in our Complete Deck Building Package. See the price tier chart below and call for deck plan availability.

Create a Professionally Designed Landscape — Landscape Plans

Many of our homes have a front-yard Landscape Plan that is complementary in design to the house plan. These comprehensive Landscape Blueprint Packages include a Frontal Sheet, Plan View, Regionalized Plant & Materials List, a sheet on Planting and Maintaining Your Landscape, Zone Maps, and a Plant Size and Description Guide. Each set of blueprints is a full 18" x 24" with clear, complete instructions in easy-to-read type. Our Landscape Plans are available with a Plant & Materials List adapted by horticultural experts to eight regions of the country. Please specify your region when ordering your plan—see region map below. Call for more information about landscape plan availability and applicable regions.

LANDSCAPE & DECK PRICE SCHEDULE

PRICE TIERS	1-SET STUDY PACKAGE	5-SET BUILDING PACKAGE	1-SET REPRODUCIBLE*	1-SET CAD*
P1	$25	$55	$145	$245
P2	$45	$75	$165	$280
P3	$75	$105	$195	$330
P4	$105	$135	$225	$385
P5	$175	$205	$405	$690
P6	$215	$245	$445	$750
D1	$45	$75**	$90	$90
D2	$75	$105**	$150	$150

PRICES SUBJECT TO CHANGE

* REQUIRES AN E-MAIL ADDRESS OR FAX NUMBER
** 3-SET BUILDING PACKAGE

BEFORE YOU ORDER

TERMS & CONDITIONS

OUR 90-DAY EXCHANGE POLICY

BUY WITH CONFIDENCE!

Hanley Wood is committed to ensuring your satisfaction with your blueprint order, which is why a we offer a 90-day exchange policy. With the exception of Reproducible Plan Package orders, we will exchange your entire first order for an equal or greater number of blueprints from our plan collection within 90 days of the original order. The entire content of your original order must be returned before an exchange will be processed. Please call our customer service department at 1-888-690-1116 for your return authorization number and shipping instructions. If the returned blueprints look used, redlined, or copied, we will not honor your exchange. Fees for exchanging your blueprints are as follows: 20% of the amount of the original order, plus the difference in cost if exchanging for a design in a higher price bracket or less the difference in cost if exchanging for a design in a lower price bracket. (Because they can be copied, Reproducible blueprints are not exchangeable or refundable.) Please call for current postage and handling prices. Shipping and handling charges are not refundable.

ARCHITECTURAL AND ENGINEERING SEALS

Some cities and states now require that a licensed architect or engineer review and "seal" a blueprint, or officially approve it, prior to construction. Prior to application for a building permit or the start of actual construction, we strongly advise that you consult your local building official who can tell you if such a review is required.

LOCAL BUILDING CODES AND ZONING REQUIREMENTS

Each plan was designed to meet or exceed the requirements of a nationally recognized model building code in effect at the time and place the plan was drawn. Typically plans designed after the year 2000 conform to the International Residential Building Code (IRC 2000 or 2003). The IRC is comprised of portions of the three major codes below. Plans drawn before 2000 conform to one of the three recognized building codes in effect at the time: Building Officials and Code Administrators (BOCA) International, Inc.;

the Southern Building Code Congress International, (SBCCI) Inc.; the International Conference of Building Officials (ICBO); or the Council of American Building Officials (CABO).

Because of the great differences in geography and climate throughout the United States and Canada, each state, county, and municipality has its own building codes, zone requirements, ordinances, and building regulations. Your plan may need to be modified to comply with local requirements. In addition, you may need to obtain permits or inspections from local governments before and in the course of construction. We authorize the use of the blueprints on the express condition that you consult a local licensed architect or engineer of your choice prior to beginning construction and strictly comply with all local building codes, zoning requirements, and other applicable laws, regulations, ordinances, and requirements. Notice: Plans for homes to be built in Nevada must be redrawn by a Nevada-registered professional. Consult your local building official for more information on this subject.

TERMS AND CONDITIONS

These designs are protected under the terms of United States Copyright Law and may not be copied or reproduced in any way, by

any means, unless you have purchased a Reproducible Plan Package and signed the accompanying license to modify and copy the plan, which clearly indicates your right to modify, copy, or reproduce. We authorize the use of your chosen design as an aid in the construction of ONE (1) single- or multifamily home only. You may not use this design to build a second dwelling or multiple dwellings without purchasing another blueprint or blueprints or paying additional design fees. Multi-use fees vary by designer—please call one of experienced sales representatives for a quote.

DISCLAIMER

The designers we work with have put substantial care and effort into the creation of their blueprints. However, because we cannot provide on-site consultation, supervision, and control over actual construction, and because of the great variance in local building requirements, building practices, and soil, seismic, weather, and other conditions, WE MAKE NO WARRANTY OF ANY KIND, EXPRESS OR IMPLIED, WITH RESPECT TO THE CONTENT OR USE OF THE BLUEPRINTS, INCLUDING BUT NOT LIMITED TO ANY WARRANTY OF MERCHANTABILITY OR OF FITNESS FOR A PARTICULAR PURPOSE. ITEMS, PRICES, TERMS, AND CONDITIONS ARE SUBJECT TO CHANGE WITHOUT NOTICE.

**CALL TOLL-FREE
1-800-521-6797
OR VISIT
EPLANS.COM**

IMPORTANT COPYRIGHT NOTICE

From the Council of Publishing Home Designers

Blueprints for residential construction (or working drawings, as they are often called in the industry) are copyrighted intellectual property, protected under the terms of the United States Copyright Law and, therefore, cannot be copied legally for use in building. The following are some guidelines to help you get what you need to build your home, without violating copyright law:

1. HOME PLANS ARE COPYRIGHTED

Just like books, movies, and songs, home plans receive protection under the federal copyright laws. The copyright laws prevent anyone, other than the copyright owner, from reproducing, modifying, or reusing the plans or design without permission of the copyright owner.

2. DO NOT COPY DESIGNS OR FLOOR PLANS FROM ANY PUBLICATION, ELECTRONIC MEDIA, OR EXISTING HOME

It is illegal to copy, change, or redraw home designs found in a plan book, CDROM or on the Internet. The right to modify plans is one of the exclusive rights of copyright. It is also illegal to copy or redraw a constructed home that is protected by copyright, even if you have never seen the plans for the home. If you find a plan or home that you like, you must purchase a set of plans from an authorized source. The plans may not be lent, given away, or sold by the purchaser.

3. DO NOT USE PLANS TO BUILD MORE THAN ONE HOUSE

The original purchaser of house plans is typically licensed to build a single home from the plans. Building more than one home from the plans without permission is an infringement of the home designer's copyright. The purchase of a multiple-set package of plans is for the construction of a single home only. The purchase of additional sets of plans does not grant the right to construct more than one home.

4. HOUSE PLANS IN THE FORM OF BLUEPRINTS OR BLACKLINES CANNOT BE COPIED OR REPRODUCED

Plans, blueprints, or blacklines, unless they are reproducibles, cannot be copied or reproduced without prior written consent of the copyright owner. Copy shops and blueprinters are prohibited from making copies of these plans without the copyright release letter you receive with reproducible plans.

5. HOUSE PLANS IN THE FORM OF BLUEPRINTS OR BLACKLINES CANNOT BE REDRAWN

Plans cannot be modified or redrawn without first obtaining the copyright owner's permission. With your purchase of plans, you are licensed to make non-structural changes by "red-lining" the purchased plans. If you need to make structural changes or need to redraw the plans for any reason, you must purchase a reproducible set of plans (see topic 6) which includes a license to modify the plans. Blueprints do not come with a license to make structural changes or to redraw the plans. You may not reuse or sell the modified design.

6. REPRODUCIBILE HOME PLANS

Reproducible plans (for example sepias, mylars, CAD files, electronic files, and vellums) come with a license to make modifications to the plans. Once modified, the plans can be taken to a local copy shop or blueprinter to make up to 10 or 12 copies of the plans to use in the construction of a single home. Only one home can be constructed from any single purchased set of reproducible plans either in original form or as modified. The license to modify and copy must be completed and returned before the plan will be shipped.

7. MODIFIED DESIGNS CANNOT BE REUSED

Even if you are licensed to make modifications to a copyrighted design, the modified design is not free from the original designer's copyright. The sale or reuse of the modified design is prohibited. Also, be aware that any modification to plans relieves the original designer from liability for design defects and voids all warranties expressed or implied.

8. WHO IS RESPONSIBLE FOR COPYRIGHT INFRINGEMENT?

Any party who participates in a copyright violation may be responsible including the purchaser, designers, architects, engineers, drafters, homeowners, builders, contractors, sub-contractors, copy shops, blueprinters, developers, and real estate agencies. It does not matter whether or not the individual knows that a violation is being committed. Ignorance of the law is not a valid defense.

9. PLEASE RESPECT HOME DESIGN COPYRIGHTS

In the event of any suspected violation of a copyright, or if there is any uncertainty about the plans purchased, the publisher, architect, designer, or the Council of Publishing Home Designers (www.cphd.org) should be contacted before proceeding. Awards are sometimes offered for information about home design copyright infringement.

10. PENALTIES FOR INFRINGEMENT

Penalties for violating a copyright may be severe. The responsible parties are required to pay actual damages caused by the infringement (which may be substantial), plus any profits made by the infringer commissions to include all profits from the sale of any home built from an infringing design. The copyright law also allows for the recovery of statutory damages, which may be as high as $150,000 for each infringement. Finally, the infringer may be required to pay legal fees which often exceed the damages.

BLUEPRINT PRICE SCHEDULE

PRICE TIERS	1-SET STUDY PACKAGE	5-SET BUILDING PACKAGE	8-SET BUILDING PACKAGE	1-SET REPRODUCIBLE*	1-SET CAD*
A1	$470	$520	$575	$700	$1,055
A2	$510	$565	$620	$765	$1,230
A3	$575	$630	$690	$870	$1,400
A4	$620	$685	$750	$935	$1,570
C1	$665	$740	$810	$1,000	$1,735
C2	$715	$795	$855	$1,065	$1,815
C3	$785	$845	$910	$1,145	$1,915
C4	$840	$915	$970	$1,225	$2,085
L1	$930	$1,030	$1,115	$1,390	$2,500
L2	$1,010	$1,105	$1,195	$1,515	$2,575
L3	$1,115	$1,220	$1,325	$1,665	$2,835
L4	$1,230	$1,350	$1,440	$1,850	$3,140
SQ1				$0.40/SQ. FT.	$0.68/SQ. FT.
SQ3				$0.55/SQ. FT.	$0.94/SQ. FT.
SQ5				$0.80/SQ. FT	$1.36/SQ. FT.
SQ7				$1.00/SQ. FT.	$1.70/SQ. FT.
SQ9				$1.25/SQ. FT.	$2.13/SQ. FT.
SQ11				$1.50/SQ. FT.	$2.55/SQ. FT.

PRICES SUBJECT TO CHANGE

* REQUIRES AN E-MAIL ADDRESS OR FAX NUMBER

PLAN #	PRICE TIER	PAGE	MATERIALS LIST	DECK	DECK PRICE	LANDSCAPE	LANDSCAPE PRICE	REGIONS
HPK3300001	SQ1	4	Y					
HPK3300033	C4	8						
HPK3300034	C1	12	Y					
HPK3300035	A4	13						
HPK3300036	A3	13						
HPK3300037	A3	14	Y					
HPK3300038	A3	15	Y					
HPK3300039	A3	16	Y					
HPK3300040	A3	17	Y					
HPK3300041	A3	18	Y					
HPK3300042	A2	19	Y					
HPK3300043	A3	19	Y					
HPK3300044	A2	20						
HPK3300045	A2	21						
HPK3300046	A3	22	Y					
HPK3300047	A4	23						
HPK3300048	A3	24						
HPK3300049	A3	25						
HPK3300050	A3	26						
HPK3300051	A4	27						
HPK3300052	A3	28		OLA004	P3	123568		
HPK3300053	A4	29	Y					
HPK3300054	A3	30	Y					
HPK3300055	A3	30						
HPK3300056	A4	31						
HPK3300057	A3	32	Y					
HPK3300058	A3	33						
HPK3300059	A4	34	Y					
HPK3300060	A3	34	Y					
HPK3300061	A4	35	Y					
HPK3300062	A4	36	Y					
HPK3300063	A4	37	Y					
HPK3300064	A4	38	Y					
HPK3300065	A4	39	Y					
HPK3300066	A4	40	Y					
HPK3300067	A4	41	Y					
HPK3300068	A4	42	Y					
HPK3300069	A4	43	Y					
HPK3300070	A3	43	Y					
HPK3300071	A3	44	Y					
HPK3300072	A3	44	Y					
HPK3300073	A4	45	Y					
HPK3300074	A4	46	Y					
HPK3300075	A4	47	Y					
HPK3300076	A4	48	Y					
HPK3300077	A4	49	Y					
HPK3300078	A4	49	Y					
HPK3300079	A4	50						
HPK3300080	A3	51						
HPK3300081	A3	52						
HPK3300082	A3	53						
HPK3300083	A3	54						
HPK3300084	A4	55						
HPK3300085	A4	56						
HPK3300086	C3	57	Y					
HPK3300087	A3	58						
HPK3300088	A3	59						
HPK3300089	A3	60						
HPK3300090	A3	61						
HPK3300091	A4	62						
HPK3300092	A4	63						
HPK3300093	A3	63	Y					
HPK3300094	A3	64						
HPK3300095	A3	64	Y					
HPK3300096	A3	65						
HPK3300097	A2	66	Y					
HPK3300098	A2	67	Y					
HPK3300099	A2	68	Y					
HPK3300100	A3	68	Y					
HPK3300101	A3	69	Y					
HPK3300102	A3	70	Y					
HPK3300103	A3	70	Y					
HPK3300002	A3	71						
HPK3300104	A3	72	Y					
HPK3300105	A3	73						
HPK3300106	A2	73						
HPK3300107	A2	74	Y					
HPK3300108	A3	74						

ORDER BLUEPRINTS 24 HOURS, 7 DAYS A WEEK, AT 1-800-521-6797 OR EPLANS.COM

Left table:

PLAN #	PRICE TIER	PAGE	MATERIALS LIST	DECK	DECK PRICE	LANDSCAPE	LANDSCAPE PRICE	REGIONS
HPK3300109	A4	75	Y			OLA001	P3	123568
HPK3300110	A4	76	Y	ODA013	D1	OLA001	P3	123568
HPK3300111	A4	77	Y	ODA013	D1	OLA001	P3	123568
HPK3300112	A3	78	Y	ODA015	D1	OLA027	P3	12345678
HPK3300113	A4	78	Y	ODA014	D1	OLA037	P4	347
HPK3300114	A3	79	Y	ODA018	D2	OLA026	P3	1234568
HPK3300115	A4	80	Y			OLA088	P4	12345678
HPK3300116	A3	81	Y					
HPK3300117	A2	82	Y					
HPK3300118	A2	82	Y					
HPK3300119	A2	83	Y					
HPK3300120	A2	84	Y					
HPK3300121	A2	85	Y					
HPK3300122	A3	86	Y					
HPK3300123	A3	87	Y					
HPK3300124	A2	88						
HPK3300125	A3	88						
HPK3300126	A3	89						
HPK3300127	A3	90	Y					
HPK3300003	A3	90						
HPK3300128	A4	91						
HPK3300129	A3	92						
HPK3300130	A2	93	Y					
HPK3300131	A3	94	Y					
HPK3300132	A4	95	Y					
HPK3300133	A2	96	Y					
HPK3300134	A3	96	Y					
HPK3300135	A2	97	Y					
HPK3300136	A3	97	Y					
HPK3300137	A3	98	Y					
HPK3300138	A3	98	Y					
HPK3300139	C1	99						
HPK3300004	A4	99	Y					
HPK3300140	A4	100	Y					
HPK3300141	C1	102	Y					
HPK3300142	C2	103	Y					
HPK3300143	C1	104	Y					
HPK3300144	C1	104	Y					
HPK3300145	C1	105	Y					
HPK3300146	C2	105	Y					
HPK3300147	C1	106	Y					
HPK3300148	C1	107	Y					
HPK3300149	C1	108	Y					
HPK3300150	C1	109	Y					
HPK3300151	C1	110	Y					
HPK3300152	C1	110	Y					
HPK3300153	C1	111	Y					
HPK3300154	C1	112	Y					
HPK3300155	C1	112	Y					
HPK3300156	C4	113	Y					
HPK3300157	C4	114	Y					
HPK3300158	C4	115	Y					
HPK3300159	C4	116	Y					
HPK3300160	C4	117	Y					
HPK3300162	C4	118						
HPK3300163	C4	119						
HPK3300164	C1	120						
HPK3300165	C3	120	Y					
HPK3300166	A4	121						
HPK3300167	C1	122						
HPK3300168	C3	123						
HPK3300169	A4	124	Y					
HPK3300170	C1	125						
HPK3300171	C2	126	Y					
HPK3300172	C2	127	Y					
HPK3300173	A4	128						
HPK3300174	A4	129	Y					
HPK3300175	A4	129	Y					
HPK3300176	SQ1	130	Y					

Right table:

PLAN #	PRICE TIER	PAGE	MATERIALS LIST	DECK	DECK PRICE	LANDSCAPE	LANDSCAPE PRICE	REGIONS
HPK3300177	C1	131						
HPK3300178	A4	131	Y					
HPK3300179	A4	132	Y					
HPK3300180	C1	133	Y					
HPK3300181	C1	134	Y					
HPK3300182	C1	135	Y					
HPK3300183	C1	136	Y					
HPK3300184	C2	137	Y					
HPK3300185	C2	138	Y			OLA001	P3	123568
HPK3300186	A4	139	Y	ODA025	D2	OLA037	P4	347
HPK3300187	C2	140	Y			OLA038	P3	7
HPK3300188	A4	141	Y			OLA001	P3	123568
HPK3300189	A4	142	Y			OLA010	P3	1234568
HPK3300190	A4	143	Y					
HPK3300191	C1	144	Y	ODA012	D2	OLA010	P3	1234568
HPK3300192	C1	145	Y	ODA006	D1	OLA021	P3	123568
HPK3300193	C1	146	Y			OLA037	P4	347
HPK3300194	C1	147	Y			OLA001	P3	123568
HPK3300195	C2	147	Y			OLA018	P3	12345678
HPK3300196	C1	148	Y					
HPK3300197	C1	149						
HPK3300198	A4	150						
HPK3300199	A4	150						
HPK3300200	A4	151						
HPK3300201	C1	151						
HPK3300202	A4	152	Y					
HPK3300203	A4	152	Y					
HPK3300204	A4	153						
HPK3300205	A4	153						
HPK3300206	A4	154						
HPK3300207	A4	155						
HPK3300208	C1	155						
HPK3300209	C1	156				OLA005	P3	123568
HPK3300210	C1	156				OLA012	P3	12345678
HPK3300211	C1	157				OLA004	P3	123568
HPK3300212	A4	158	Y					
HPK3300213	SQ1	158	Y					
HPK3300214	A4	159	Y					
HPK3300215	C1	160						
HPK3300216	C1	161				OLA008	P4	1234568
HPK3300217	A4	162	Y					
HPK3300218	A4	163						
HPK3300219	C1	163						
HPK3300220	A4	164						
HPK3300221	A4	165						
HPK3300222	C1	166	Y			OLA001	P3	123568
HPK3300223	C1	167	Y					
HPK3300224	A4	168	Y					
HPK3300225	A4	169						
HPK3300226	A4	169						
HPK3300227	C3	170	Y					
HPK3300228	L1	172	Y					
HPK3300229	C3	173	Y			OLA038	P3	7
HPK3300230	C2	173	Y					
HPK3300231	C3	174	Y					
HPK3300232	C3	174	Y					
HPK3300233	C4	175						
HPK3300234	C1	175	Y			OLA010	P3	1234568
HPK3300235	C3	176	Y					
HPK3300236	C3	176	Y					
HPK3300237	C2	177	Y					
HPK3300238	C2	177	Y					
HPK3300239	C2	178	Y					
HPK3300240	C4	179						
HPK3300241	SQ1	180	Y					
HPK3300242	C1	180	Y					
HPK3300243	C3	181						
HPK3300244	C1	192						

The American Collection

Ranch-style homes have come a long way, yet they haven't lost their original charm or appeal. This home, for example, uses clerestory dormers, a long covered porch, and front-facing gables to add country character to a basic ranch design. Other houses in this collection also borrow elements from varying styles to elevate the ranch into an inviting, attractive, expressive home. See more of this plan on page 41.